My Life, My Angel

A Story of Enduring All Things Through the Power of
Faith, Hope, and Love

Louise "Lady L." Buckner

Impactful Book

My Life, My Angel / Louise Buckner
ISBN-13: 978-1-945793-62-2
ISBN-10: 1-945793-62-7

Special thanks to:

John Westly Buckner

Dorothy Mae Webb-Smith

Solomon Smith Sr.

Essie Mae Buckner

Eddie Rogers (my Auntie Mae)

Ella Mae Moss

Mother Willie Love

Robert James Buckner Sr.

Donald Hudson Sr.

Rev. Robert L. Buckner

LaKeshia Melissa Buckner-Smith

Darnell Westly Buckner

Mr. and Mrs. Charles Taylor

Rev. Dr. Oscar T. Moses

Eric L. Robinson (photo credit)

CONTENTS

PREFACE

These words are a look at life and its circle of days, months, and years. These pages are written to enlighten the skeptics concerning love and its endless pursuit of the heart by introducing them to my family. I have also included reflections and questions at the end of each chapter to help you glean from my life experiences and grow in your walk with God.

In this book, I aim to tell the story of our struggles and our successes, but most of all, our dependence on the Lord. Please be aware that the pages in this book contain sensitive details from my life that may be difficult for some to read. Ultimately, however, this story bears witness to God's grace and mercy, which are given to us each day.

This story shows how His love embraces our every moment of existence, and in due time—with belief—heals our heartaches and pain and brings joy to our struggles. It reveals how, by being truthful and respectful to one another, as my husband and I have been, you will find that the sky is your limit.

INTRODUCTION

The Family Dynamic

I started writing this memoir on Monday, September 15, 2003. I stood on the train platform at the LaSalle Street Station on the Metra Rock Island Suburban Line, which runs between Chicago and Joliet, Illinois, to the southwest. I was waiting for the evening train after a long day at the 311 Center, where I worked. With a prayer in my heart and memories of my past filling my mind, I began to write.

My earliest childhood memories are of living in a big white-stucco house with gray trim in Englewood, a predominately white, middle-class community at the time.

We had seven bedrooms and two bathrooms. At first, there were Mama, Daddy, Grandmama Ida (my father's mother), and my three brothers. Over the next several years, Mama gave birth to three more children; I gained two sisters and one more brother.

I remember asking Mama for another sister once, which would have given us four boys and four girls. Mama chuckled and said, "Hmmm, I am through, child, have it yourself."

When I was young, it was normal to have up to three generations living in one house. Grandparents helped keep an eye on the youngsters. The adults in the family didn't play around, either. They meant what they said, and they said what they meant. If you got "the look," it meant you better get yourself together quickly before they adjusted your attitude for you.

Believe me, you didn't want that. They believed in "spare the rod, spoil the child," and they would have none of our nonsense. This was a big problem for me.

I had a major mouth problem. My mouth was rather large and argumentative—I got some straps to my behind to prove it. Come to think of it, my mouth hasn't changed all that much since childhood.

When we got in trouble around the house, Daddy lined all seven of us up against the dining room wall and went back and forth, down the line, on our behinds. Daddy was fair to us kids, but stern. If we disobeyed after having been warned by him, out came the belt.

My Mama didn't play around, either, but she had a different way of getting that behind. She placed our head in a lock between her knees while she sat, so she had nothing but behind in front of her. Mama had a knee-lock like that of a Worldwide Wrestling Entertainment champion. I still wonder where those knees of hers came from. They held our head so tight that we could not break free.

Then there was Grandmama. She called you over to her, balled up her right hand into a tight fist, grabbed your head, and leaned it on her bosom for support. She then twisted her fist into your head, making you dizzy and giving you a headache for a long time. She called it mauling. You did not want too many of those. Grandmama's hand was powerful.

My parents and grandmother highly valued obedience, but it is important to note that this desire for good behavior came from a place of love. They had high standards for us children, and they taught us to obey the Word of God and to treat others respectfully. They hoped to spare us pain later in life by teaching us how to behave when we were still young.

My two cousins, Katie and Bertha, came to Chicago to live with us after my aunt passed away. Daddy's brother, Uncle Sam, was highly unstable, and he couldn't provide a safe haven for his children. Grandmama didn't want them to be separated from family, so the girls moved in with us.

Daddy never complained about taking care of two more children who weren't his. And he always made sure that when we went south to visit family, my cousins at least had a chance to see their daddy. I remember my daddy would drive all over town, looking for my uncle, so his kids could see him before we returned home to Chicago. Visiting my uncle was uncertain because he never stayed in one place for long. Sometimes we didn't find him until the last minute.

Being Honest

Life wasn't always easy, growing up with my cousins in the house. They were older, so they were in charge on our walks to school. On the way, they stopped at their friend's house. It was located a block from our house, on the way to school.

Their friend had a dog who always stood on the second-floor landing in the building, looking down, barking at us. I was scared of dogs, so I cried all the way to school.

One day, I got home with a note from my teacher pinned on my clothes. It said, "Louise enters my classroom every morning crying."

After my father got home, he whipped my behind as I ran up and down the sofa in the living room. I was confused, afraid of him, and afraid of my older cousins getting mad at me if I told why I cried before school.

Not too long after, I wised up. I told Daddy why I was so upset, mad, and frightened every morning.

Once he realized what was wrong with me on school days, all hell broke loose for my cousins. That was one time I was glad it all hit the fan. My cousins were blazing mad at me, but my behind was glad I had been honest with my father and avoided another whooping. No more notes and no more crying to school for me.

A Family with Character

The adults in my home were firm, but we were never abused or misused throughout our childhood. We were held accountable for our actions. We learned manners, self-respect, and respect for others.

I appreciate the character of my family. We were taught to strive to be the best at whatever task we were set to, and to be thankful for every gift God blessed us with. My parents taught us to work hard so that we could have a successful future. They certainly always had our best interests in mind, and they taught us to depend on God.

My family wasn't perfect. We had our fights and disagreements. We had our hurts and our fears. But, looking back, I can see how God used those years, the good and the bad, to mold me into the woman I am today. He has used my upbringing to shape me into a woman of character. Daddy and Mama instilled in my siblings and me virtues like honesty, loyalty, courage, and the discipline to do the right thing even when it is inconvenient. Most importantly, they taught us to follow the Lord and to live in submission to His Word.

Introduction Reflection

Read Proverbs 22:6.

Your home of origin shapes the person you become in many ways.

Louise learned the value of obedience and hard work from her parents.

What was your home like growing up? What was positive about your upbringing in teaching and molding good traits into your life? To find healing and create a better life for yourself, what hurts from those years have you had to work through?

_____

_____

_____

_____

_____

CHAPTER ONE

My Mother

My son, hear the instruction of thy father, and forsake not the law of thy mother: for they shall be an ornament of grace unto thy head, and chains about thy neck.
—***Proverbs 1:8–9***

Dorothy Mae Webb was born June 12, 1934, to Ben and Lizette Webb. The Midwest was just beginning to feel the effects of the Dust Bowl the year Mama came, but her family's home in Durant, Mississippi, did not suffer any real consequences from the deadly drought.

Mama was the youngest of six, three girls and three boys. Her mother died at an early age, leaving her father to raise his young family on his own. I never knew the circumstances behind my grandmother's premature death. I don't know much about her, possibly because Mama didn't remember much herself.

I don't recall there being any pictures of Grandmama Webb, and I often wonder what her voice sounded like. My aunts, being my mother's older sisters, told me that my first toe on my right foot was the same as my grand-mother's—it was bent. Known as a hammer toe, the bone grew down instead of outward. I like to say her steps live on through me. I hope I'm stepping in the right direction.

Mama spoke highly of her daddy. At that time, Mama said he owned acres and acres of land in Mississippi. Mama talked about how, on the weekends, the family made the trek to Sallie, Mississippi, for hours and hours of fun. She said that whatever they asked for, her father provided it.

Mama's face always lit up when she talked about her dad, just as mine does when I talk about her.

My mother was part Navajo. She was blessed with a beautiful olive skin tone, high cheekbones, long, flowing hair, strong, fine legs, a soul-sister shape, and a soft speak-ing voice. Because she had to grow up without a mother to teach her, Mama didn't know a thing about cooking when she and Daddy first got married, so Grandmama taught her.

Cooking and baking were an all-day job back then. Mama practically lived in the kitchen, baking the daily biscuits and preparing meals for her growing family. When Mama was still learning to make biscuits the way Daddy liked them, she had to make them again and again until she got them right. As I got older, she taught me how to follow the recipe, and we made them together.

I remember my mother as an amazing cook. She could whip up something delicious out of whatever we had in the house. Whatever she created, it was always on time for dinner. And her desserts were incredible! The peach cobbler dripping with sugar and butter in the summer was delicious. And her rice pudding, bread pudding, and banana pudding were the best on the block!

But her signature dish was her turkey and dressing and homemade cheeseburgers, which she served on Sundays. If there was one dish Daddy loved, it was Mama's turkey and dressing. The aroma of that dish filled the house. If Daddy was stressed or giving Mama the cold shoulder, she made turkey and dressing to pull him out of his mood.

At Sunday dinner, my siblings and I all sat around the table while watching my parents' bedroom door, trying not to burst out laughing, because we knew the drill.

Mama said, "Pat" (the name she called my father sometimes); then she called him again, "Pat, come on and eat."

He'd reply, "I ain't eating."

This went back and forth three or four times. Our eyes, all fourteen of them, stared at the bedroom door, almost counting the seconds until it opened. It never failed. Daddy made his way out of the room, not making eye contact with any of us; then he went to the washroom to clean up before coming to the table.

While he was doing that, we were hardly breathing as we kicked the feet next to ours or knocked each other's knees. We all knew darn well we'd better not laugh.

Daily Chores

Mama was my rock throughout my growing up. As the second-oldest and the first girl, I had plenty of responsibilities, like helping to make the daily biscuits. I also had to help with the laundry twice a week, three to four loads each time. We couldn't afford an electric washer and dryer, so everything had to be done by hand. We had an old washing machine with the manual wringer on the top front of it that we had to crank to remove the excess water from the clothes. Afterward, we hung the clothes to dry on a line with clothespins. We hung clothes from front to back and from side to side of the basement during the winter months.

Mama and I always looked forward to spring and summertime, when we could hang the laundry in the backyard to dry in the sun and let the breeze blow through them. God's air was so refreshing, bringing a welcome break from being cooped up indoors. At those times, I felt joyful, both because I was able to spend time in God's beautiful creation and because of how I could share these special moments with my mother.

When Mama wasn't cooking, cleaning, washing, and paying bills, she was taking care of her seven children, and I often worked shoulder to shoulder with her. We taught my young siblings to count, and we showed them how to tie their shoes. We helped with their homework and taught them how to tell time.

My mama might not have had the chance to know her mother, or to learn from her how to keep a home while she was growing up, but she worked hard to make sure her own children didn't grow up without learning how to take care of themselves and their future families.

Easter Frocks

The girls in our house were not allowed to wear pants while I was growing up. The first thing I did when I got home from school was change out of my school dress and into something I could do my chores in. I owned three school dresses. On Mondays and Wednesdays, I wore dress number one. On Tuesdays and Thursdays, I wore dress number two. Dress number three was for Fridays. I repeated that sequence every week.

Whenever Mama told my father that we needed shoes or clothes, he went shopping for seven kids at one time. It was crowded in the store, so Daddy measured us at home. He measured our feet by tracing them on a piece of paper and put each of our names by our feet outlines. He used a string to measure us girls from the shoulder to just below the knee, and he placed a knot in the string so he could recognize each child from tallest to the shortest. My brothers were measured from the shoulder to the waist for shirts and from waist to ankle for their pants.

Before Easter, both Mama and Daddy went shopping for our Easter frocks. Upon my parents' return, we girls were given dresses, hats, gloves, patent leather shoes, and purses. My siblings and I were thrilled! I walked back and forth all afternoon and evening admiring my sisters' and my new outfits. I loved how fresh the clothes smelled and how crisp they looked.

On the Sunday before Easter, Mama washed and pressed our hair using brown paper bags made into strips. She wrapped our damp hair around the paper and tied it up tight. The next morning, we had curls.

My mother was a deacon's wife, so she often wore white as a mother of the church. Church mothers were members of good standing in the church and were responsible for mentoring and assisting the younger women.

They also oversaw church functions and helped the pastor and his family, when needed.

Most of the time, my mother sat in the front row. She loved big wide hats, tailored suits, and very tall high heels to show off her nice legs. Every now and then, she sang a solo, mostly acapella. I will always remember this time in my young life while being raised in the church.

Walking with Mama

Mama didn't drive, and this was fully by her choice. Daddy used to tell the story about trying to teach her how to drive. A small animal darted out into the road in front of the car. Mama didn't want to hit it, so she panicked. That was the end of Mama driving.

If Mama had an errand to run while Daddy was working, she walked. We often walked together through Englewood, talking about life's ups and downs and the joys and disappointments of our journeys so far.

Back in the day, these neighborhoods were middle class, alive and vibrant. We could clear our minds as we took our time strolling down Seventy-First Street, Sixty-Ninth, and Seventh Streets. As we made our monthly rounds to pay the mortgage, life insurance, light, and gas bills, we talked about how we could better ourselves for the good of mankind, and especially for our Lord and Savior, Jesus Christ.

In the spring and summer, we made a pit stop to the flower shop just over the expressway at Seventy-First and State Streets. Roses were Mama's favorite. She got one or two bushes every year to plant in the backyard. The rose garden was off-limits during playtime. We all knew better than to mess around or play ball anywhere near her pride and joy! These flowers were a beautiful reminder of God's faithfulness. As I will discuss in a later chapter, I have inherited Mama's passion for gardening, and roses never fail to remind me of her.

First Lady of the House

One of Mama's greatest challenges in the home and in her marriage was her mother-in-law. In many ways, Grandmama wanted to be the first lady of the house. I remember days when Daddy returned home from a long day at work to complaints from Grandmama that Mama didn't do this right or that right. This resulted in Daddy losing his temper and taking it out on Mama. As a child, I didn't know what domestic violence was, or how to label this terrible thing that was happening in my home.

It was forbidden to talk about the dark red marks around Mama's neck, or the bruises on her body, or the tears filling her eyes. I did the best I could to be a comfort for my mother each time this happened—but it should have never happened to begin with. Mama had no one to turn to during that time, but she never once wavered in her responsibilities to her children or her husband.

We prayed that things would change, and that Mama would be happier, and her life would be fulfilled. In a few years, Grandmama became ill. Despite everything my grandmother had put her through, Mama took care of Grandmama as if she were her own mother, right up until the day the Lord called Grandmama home. God used that time to open Daddy's eyes to what a beautiful and compassionate wife he had.

When I think of a strong and beautiful woman, Mama is the first to come to mind. She was criticized a lot, but she kept moving forward, most of the time carrying heavy burdens. I never once heard her gossip or bad-mouth God's children. Her favorite song lyrics were: "Lord, don't move the mountain, but give me the strength to climb," and He did just that for her.

Chapter One Reflection

Read Romans 12:21.

Lord, don't move the mountain, but give me the strength to climb.

Mama faced some seemingly insurmountable mountains in her own mother's early death, the harsh criticism of her mother-in-law, and the abuse of her husband*, yet through the Lord's strength, she continued to love those who hurt her and eventually was honored for her gracious spirit.

(*If you are in an abusive relationship, please seek help and counsel and remove yourself from the situation. God does not desire anyone to be a victim of domestic violence).

What mountains of difficulty are you facing? How can you overcome evil circumstances or unkind people with the goodness and love of God flowing through your life?

_____

CHAPTER TWO

Grandmama

Ida Culbert was born on September 2, 1903. This was the year of the first World Series and the Wright Brothers' first powered flight. Ford Motors and Harley-Davidson were also formed in the year of her birth.

Ida was married at age 13 to Robert Smith. They had four sons before my grandfather got sick and died at the age of 25, leaving her to raise her boys alone.

Daddy's family didn't have much growing up. He often spoke about the days when they only had cornbread and milk to eat, and how Grandmama drank sweet water and ate a bit of bread, sacrificing her own belly to feed her sons.

My father vowed to take care of his mother when he was old enough. It was a promise he kept.

A Calming Voice

Grandmama was firm, and her punishment was swift

when called for, but she loved her family deeply. Before coming to live with us, she told my daddy she wanted to take me and raise me because she'd never had a daughter of her own.

Daddy said no because he wanted his children to grow up together in the same house.

I was in first or second grade the day President Kennedy was assassinated. I remember being too scared to go home after school officials announced the assassination over the loudspeaker. Most of the kids in my class, including me, thought we'd be shot too if we left that room. My teacher was very gentle with our young minds. She assured us that we were all safe, but I could see the sadness in her eyes as she tried to reassure us.

I shared my fear of being shot with Grandmama when my siblings and I got home. She talked to us briefly about how not all people are nice and some of them don't do the right things to others.

A few years after this shooting, my parents and grandparents were speaking about a civil rights leader named Dr. King Jr., who was marching on Sixty-Third and Halsted, not too far from our house. This area was considered the downtown, right in the business district of Englewood. It was known for retail stores such as Robert Hall and Three Sisters, where my family often shopped for our new clothes.

My grandma believed in Dr. King and his leadership. She said he was going to play a major part in bringing justice for us folks. She talked about the march, and how there might be trouble from people who didn't think things needed to change. I'm not sure if it was only my childhood imaginings or if we were really that close to the march, but it seemed as though I could hear Dr. King's voice and the crowd from where we lived.

I remember asking Grandmama if the crowd was coming to get us and destroy our home. Grandmama got very quiet as she looked around. She said, "No, he is not coming to harm anyone, sister."

Dr. King went on for a while, speaking very loudly, preaching and marching for people of color, demanding, peacefully, justice for all.

When Dr. King was shot and killed in April 1968, I found myself again talking about violence. I didn't understand the anger and violence going on around me. I just knew I was scared.

Grandmama and the Church

Our small church, Southern Mount Zion, rented space in a building that also included housing apartments, a Masonic Temple, and a ballroom, complete with marble features, that was located on the top level.

Most of the songs we sang came from the hymnal *Gospel Pearls,* songs like, "I Love the Lord, He Heard My Cry," "I'm on the Battlefield for My Lord," and "'Til the Old Ship of Zion." Grandmama's favorite song was "Amazing Grace." She sang this song faithfully and often away from church.

Grandmama was an older mother of the Mother's Board. As an older mother, Grandmama had a gathering of women church members and close friends who came over for quilting evenings. While making quilts, the women talked about family, current events, church, and how good God was. They were proud women with backbone and integrity, something I feel some of us lack nowadays.

Her guests laughed and talked for a few hours each week. They came around seven and left around nine in the evening. I was young, but I sometimes got a chance to join them. It was relaxing, and I could be creative in my quilting designs. It took several weeks for Grandmama and the ladies to complete one quilt. Each was a work of art to look at.

Grandmama draped each one of our beds with these labors of love. Back then, I had no idea of the value of these precious quilts, which are irreplaceable. We used these quilts on a daily basis, like ordinary blankets or comforters. So, after a while, with the washing and everyday usage, they wore out and were eventually thrown away. It saddens me to think that they are lost now; these quilts would be invaluable treasures from my grandmother if they still existed.

Grandmama's Final Years

After a while, Grandmama began to have stomach problems. This illness went on for some time. We were fortunate to have a private physician who made house calls. He came once or twice a week to see after my grandmother and drain her stomach of fluid. As time progressed, due to her illness, she was occasionally taken to the hospital by private ambulance.

My siblings and I were too young to stay at home or

visit her upstairs in the hospital, so we sat near the nurses' station. All the staff got to know us as "the Smiths," and we got candy from time to time from the nurses. I remember we looked forward to the candy.

Unfortunately, Grandmama's health didn't get any better; she wasn't coming home like before. I was almost twelve when she passed on to heaven. This was the first time that we all took a trip to Mississippi by automobile. It was a whole caravan that made its way down the highway to Grandmama's hometown. I'd never experienced anything like this firsthand. I learned that this was her request: to go back to the town where she was born and be laid to rest on the grounds of the small, white wooden church in the Smith woods—and to have her favorite song, "Amazing Grace," played at her funeral.

For this thing I besought the Lord thrice, that it might depart from me.

And he said unto me, My grace is sufficient for thee: for my strength is made perfect in weakness. Mostly gladly therefore will I rather glory in my infirmities, that the power of Christ may rest upon me.
                                   —2 Corinthians 12:8–9

Shortly after Grandmama's passing, the church moved to a larger space. In this new space, the church experienced a lot of growth in attendance, and the service became more upbeat. Another church, Sardis Missionary Baptist, with Reverend Elijah and First Lady Essie Mae Buckner, joined in with us at Southern Mount Zion M.B. Church. I didn't know it just yet, but this family would become a godsend to me.

WORKBOOK

Chapter Two Reflection

Read Ephesians 5:19.

Praise should characterize the life of a believer.

The song "Amazing Grace" was special to Grandmama, a testimony of her life, and it became the song Louise most associated with her.

What favorite hymn or Christian song best describes your walk with God? Why is this song meaningful to you?

_____

_____

_____

_____

_____

_____

CHAPTER THREE

Daddy

Solomon Smith was born January 11, 1927, in Mississippi, just four months before Lindbergh made his famous trans-Atlantic flight.

After his daddy died, it was just Grandmama, Daddy, Uncle Sam, Uncle Willie, and Uncle Jesse. Of all my uncles, Uncle Jesse stood out to me the most, because he lived in Chicago. We saw a lot of him, and he took time out with me and my siblings. I'll always remember his upbeat and refreshing look at life. His ideas were his choice—whether others approved or disapproved, it made no difference to him.

Growing up, Daddy refused to walk around with lowered eyes. His refusal to be subservient resulted in the local white folks labeling him "that bad nigger," and it caused him some trouble. Once Daddy was old enough, he enlisted in the army and headed off to serve our country. At some point, while he was still young, he joined the Masonic Order.

Daddy was a straight-up, no-nonsense person with a big heart, willing to help anyone who might need him. His knowledge and memory were sharp. He was also a man of God who loved the Bible, a passion that guided his life.

Growing up with so little had taught Daddy the value of saving for a rainy day. Many of his sayings revolved around the importance of setting something aside for later.

He said things like "Make a little bit, save a little bit," or "When you work, put some up and you will always have something to fall back on."

Besides saving money, Daddy believed in having life insurance. He said it was a shame when you had to be sorry twice, once that your loved one was gone and twice when you had to pass the hat to bury them.

He was a hard worker, my daddy. Besides working his full-time job, he also had a catering business on the side, selling BBQ, homemade cakes, and homemade ice cream. Though he used to joke about working so hard just to feed us seven kids, he was fond of saying, "Got to have steps in the door. You got to make something happen to take care of your family."

Daddy made more money in one day than others made in one week. I know—I was the timekeeper. Every week, the two of us sat down and worked out the numbers.

Because he worked so many long hours, there were weeks when Daddy was too tired to go to church on Sunday. However, he left money on the dining room table each Saturday night, separated out in seven sections, for each of us kids to pick up on the way out to put in the collection plate. As we grew, the amount he gave to us to tithe grew, too. Daddy worked hard every day, but we all knew it was God who blessed his paycheck.

My daddy once said his mailbox had turned green. He stated that if you did right by people, which, for him, included taking care of his mother after she got ill, then the Lord surely would bless you. Because of God's blessing, our family didn't want for much.

The Provider

My daddy shopped in the wholesale houses, fish markets, and fruit markets for our food. The kids in our neighborhood made fun of us because we brought home our groceries in cases instead of bags.

Chicken, neck bones, cereal, candy, hula hoops, bats and balls—whatever it was, if Daddy could buy it in bulk, he did.

He went to the vegetable stand or he drove out of the city to bring back Crowder peas by the bushels, greens by the crates, and ears of corn by the sacks. The sight of all these vegetables meant one thing: hard work.

Of course, some family members got away with less work than others. In a way, though, these times around the table shelling peas, shucking corn, and picking greens while laughing and talking were some of the best bonding moments with my family.

Just Daddy and Me

I have fond memories of me and my daddy going to the mall, just the two of us. One of the trips that stands out is the day I got my first watch. I remember feeling anxious as we walked down Sixty-Third and Halsted Streets to the jewelry store.

We had a set amount we could spend, and I wanted to make sure I picked out a watch that would last me a long time. We entered the store, and I peered through the glass case, which held a variety of watches.

I chose a Timex, known for taking a licking and keeping on ticking. It didn't matter to me that I didn't have the most expensive or fancy watch in the store. It was the thought and consideration Daddy showed me by buying me my first watch that mattered. I put the watch on right away. After sporting it all that day, I gently removed it and carefully placed it back in the case by my bedside until the next day.

Be thou diligent to know the state of thy flocks, and look well to thy herds.
—Proverbs 27:23

My father, a man of the Word, was a senior deacon of the church, but he also filled in other roles when needed. He served as the head advisor, a trustee, and, for a brief time, as the lead pastor.

I still remember some of the meetings Daddy was part of. Some took place after church, some took place over the phone, and some took place at our house. I learned at a young age about church politics, and that not everything that goes on in the Lord's house is as it should be. I also learned that leaders of any organization sometimes have to make difficult decisions that are not always popular with others.

One of the decisions Daddy and some of the other leaders made was to move our church from the Masonic Lodge to a storefront. As I grew, so did the church. We had several pastors during this time period. Reverend Elijah Buckner was among the preachers who preached on occasion.

Although he might have fallen short at times, Daddy was committed to being a godly leader of our family and bringing up his children in the Word of God. He taught my siblings and me the importance of studying the Bible diligently and applying it to our lives.

Reflections

My daddy had lots of rules, and as the head of the house, he was the chief enforcer of them. But for all that, he was fair. He wanted us to grow up with better opportunities than he had had as a child.

His biggest requirement was that all seven of his children had to finish high school. He'd only been able to finish the third grade, so he knew how hard it was to make one's way in the world without an education. It was also his dream to see us graduate from college. Wherever we ended up, he just wanted us to be better off than he'd been.

As my father was getting older, he mellowed out. He had been tough when we were young, but he taught us the value of respect, honesty, and integrity. He also taught us how important it was to read the Word of God.

Daddy might not have always made the best choices in life, but he was always hard-working and dependable. As time went on, Daddy allowed God to change his heart as he walked with Him. He was always a good daddy and provider to all eleven of us. Only God can help us better than Daddy did.

WORKBOOK

Chapter Three Reflection

Read Romans 5:3–5.

Suffering builds and forms character.

The financial hardships he faced as a child motivated Daddy to be a hard worker and an excellent provider for his family.

What trials or difficulties from your early life have shaped your values and priorities?

_____

_____

_____

_____

_____

_____

_____

CHAPTER FOUR

My Siblings

There were seven of us kids in my family, not counting my two cousins. Solomon Jr. came first; I was next. Joseph joined the family less than a year after I was born. The last four in the family are Riley, Sarah Ruth, Johnny, and Martha. Each of my siblings had unique personalities that I loved, and I learned lessons from all of them.

The Dreamer

Solomon Smith Jr., better known as Solo, has always been a dreamer with big ideas. Soft-spoken would be a good way to describe him.

As a child, Solo became very ill with German measles, a painful and unsightly disease, to say the least. The illness caused his skin to peel off the bottoms of his feet, which impaired his walking ability for a little while. He came through after a couple of weeks and was back to his old self again.

Solo was a daredevil of sorts. We often played ball in the backyard and, inevitably, the ball flew across the fence into the neighbors' yard.

On one of those early summer days, the neighbors weren't home to help us retrieve the ball. The gate was locked, and the family dog was in the yard on watch. Solo, whom we sometimes called Mr. Quick, decided he could hop the fence and save the ball before the dog could get to him. I was convinced the dog would reach him first.

But Solo hit that fence like a track star, got the ball, and was back in our yard before that so-called guard dog ever got near him. This became a sport for my older brother, and we didn't worry when the ball flew too far. Mr. Quick retrieved it every time, and the neighbors' dog never did catch him.

A few years later, Solo got his first job at my father's cousin's neighborhood grocery store. The job required him to work four hours every Saturday. This was his first encounter with independence, making his own money, and being responsible. He had to get up and be at work on time. Solo had his mind set on going to high school to get out of the neighborhood. He decided on Dunbar Vocational. Students at this school were known as the Mighty Men. He had to take an exam, apply, and be accepted into Dunbar, because he lived outside of that school's district. After doing all that was required of him, Solo became a Mighty Man.

Daddy taught him how to drive. He bought Solo a Chevy, a two-door, champagne-colored car. Solo was on cloud nine. After a while, Daddy started wanting Solo to run us younger kids around just to get us out of his hair and give him a bit of quiet.

One day, we were all sitting around the table in the dining room when Solo came downstairs and made a beeline to the door, saying he was going out. My father replied, "You're not taking your sisters and brothers with you?"

Solo already had his hand on the door when he asked us, "Do you all want to go?" Before the six of us could answer him, he was gone, and we were left with our mouths open in disbelief. We later found out that Solo had begun courting a girl.

His social life did not get in the way of his studies. My oldest brother did very well in school and was soon headed for college. Daddy got Solo a job with him during the summer before he started college. Solo was working long hours right alongside my dad. I don't believe he got much sleep at all during that time. The money was good, but Daddy insisted on Solo opening a savings account.

One of Mama and Daddy's proudest, hardest days was the day when Solo left for college. The three of them drove to Southern Illinois University (SIU), along with Uncle Jesse. We all wrote to Solo at school from time to time. He replied when he could. His classes and activities kept him busy, and he had also joined a fraternity. I noticed his "brand" when he came home that first summer. I couldn't believe the pain he'd willingly endured to be a part of that group.

In all things shewing thyself a pattern of good works: in doctrine shewing uncorruptness. gravity, sincerity...
—Titus 2:7

After finishing college, Solo returned home to Chicago and started to work. It was not long after that he found the love of his life, Nancy. They married and had three girls. Solo and his wife started a catering and bakery business. Solo is still a big dreamer and entrepreneur today. He has the heart of a servant and is very involved in his temple, where he loves to teach and talk with others about God's Word.

The Adventurer

Joseph, better known as Joe, can talk to anybody for hours; a quick errand for the rest of us could take him all day. Because we were born so close together, he liked to joke that we were twins. For two weeks out of every year, we're both the same age. Then my birthday comes around, and I'm a year older than he is again.

Joe's an adventurer. Where Solomon would make a plan and run for it, Joe would keep you wondering what his next move would be.

He had quite the talent for drawing when we were kids. Even though he never had any training, he entered drawing contests and won.

He's also a joker—don't try to breathe or eat when he's on a roll—and a music lover. As kids, we made box guitars out of shoe boxes. We'd cut out a hole in the box and use rubber bands for our strings. We had no knowledge in music notes or chords. But we knew about having fun, and a lot of fun we had.

As Joe got older, his love for music grew, too. It didn't

matter the sound or the genre, Joe listened to it. His album collection was so massive that his closet was in danger of collapsing from the weight of the wax. He could also tell you all about the artists and the songs. To this day, his head is like an encyclopedia of music from the 1970s and on. He's the same way with cars.

As the family adventurer, he was the first of us kids to ever fly in a plane. I was in awe of the idea of him stepping onto the aircraft and leaving his hometown to follow an adventure in California. I couldn't wait for him to come home and tell me all about his trip.

He and Mama had a special bond. She would call him Joe Baby, and if she needed him to do something, he'd respond with "I got you, babe," or "What can I do for you?" or "You need my undivided attention?" or "I'm listening."

A merry heart maketh a cheerful countenance: but by the sorrow of the heart the spirit is broken.

All the days of the afflicted are evil: but he that is of a merry heart hath a continual feast.
—Proverbs 15:13, 15

Joe is one of the world's oldest teenagers. His body has aged, but his soul is as young as ever. The best part is, he makes you feel young when you're around him, too.

Joe has one daughter, Cirena, who is the love of his life.

Big Daddy

Riley, better known as Big Daddy, was always work-ing on something around the house. One of our neighbors was a laborer, and Riley, a wide-eyed young lad, was tak-ing note. Nothing was off-limits to my brother when it came to working with his hands. We started calling him Bachur, which was our made-up name that meant, "Are you sure you know what you're doing?" Riley just went on about fixing things, paying no mind to what we called him.

If Daddy called a repairman to work on something, Ri-ley was right on that person's heels, watching their every move. He learned so many things just by paying attention. He became a great repairman. As time went on, he took his self-taught talents to the streets. He built up a clientele of people from all walks of life, including me. He was the boiler man, plumber, carpenter, and painter.

When Riley wasn't tinkering with a repair, you could find him in the kitchen. As teenagers, we perfected a brownie recipe that everyone in the family looked forward to. And if Daddy needed an extra pair of hands with his catering business, Riley was there.

He spent more time in the kitchen as Mama and Dad began to get up in years. If a family member needed a re-fresher on family recipes, he was the go-to person. Favorite recipes included pound cake and homemade ice cream. Once I got out of that house, or, should I say, out of that kitchen, I was not eager to cook at my own home. When the time came, he became Mama and Daddy's pri-mary caregiver.

I have shewed you all things. How that so laboring ye ought to support the weak, and to remember the words of the Lord Jesus, how he said, it is more blessed to give than to receive.

—Acts 20:35

Outside of his work and caring for our parents, Riley served as the president of the usher board at Good Hope Missionary Baptist for many years. It was a position he took seriously. His pastor said that Riley was the church's cheerleader. His voice was loud and clear when songs of praise were sung and when the Word was being preached.

Riley never married, and he had no children.

The Social Butterfly

Sarah Ruth was nicknamed Niky by Daddy. To this day, I don't know why. If there are two things she loves, it's talking fashion and eating cake. She's not a fan of watermelon.

She was born in the summer, when it was hot, so, on one of her birthdays, instead of baking her a cake, Daddy got her two nice watermelons. He placed them in the deep freezer to chill for a few hours, and then, later in the day, Daddy called everyone to the table to sing "Happy Birthday" around the watermelons. I think—no, I take that back, I know—that to this day, that's the reason she cannot get enough cake.

Mama often dressed Sarah Ruth and Martha up in matching dresses and jumpers growing up. Sarah became a little social butterfly. Not shy or timid around others, she grew in popularity.

Growing up, she liked "shopping" in the wish books, another name we had for magazines back in the day. I recall how we—me, Mama, and my sisters—looked through the wish books every Saturday while we did our nails around the dining room table. This was a Mama-and-daughters ritual. Mind you, during that time, we could not shop out of those books; it was not in our budget.

Once she was old enough to work, Sarah Ruth got a job at Englewood Hospital. She never stopped working, or shopping, after that. She is a "shop 'til you drop" kind of girl, not only for herself, but for others, too. Through her hard work, her wishes became a reality. I relied on her for her fashion awareness. Every season, I asked her what the latest colors and fashion styles were for the upcoming year.

> *For the law having a shadow of good things to come, and not the very image of the things, can never with those sacrifices which they offered year by year continually make the comers thereunto perfect.*
> **—Hebrews 10:1**

Education is very important to Sarah. She is always advocating for young people's betterment through education, because she wants the best out of our youth. I think my sister lives her life to encourage the best out of the youth in our community. She also prays for the families she knows, name by name.

Sarah married twice and had two sons, Willie and

Denzel. Today, she enjoys being a grandmother, talking up a storm, shopping on every network, and enjoying cake whenever possible.

The Performer

Johnny is my third brother and the sixth child in our family. Mama called him Bunny, and as a baby, he would wail if a man tried to hold him. Once a woman took him, the crying stopped.

All three of my brothers shared the same birth month. One year, when Johnny was about two years old, Daddy decided to make a combined birthday cake for the three of them. The thirteen layers of jelly and coconut cake seemed to tower over my daddy. I remember Daddy beaming as everyone admired his creation. Little Johnny was amazed by the tall cake he got to share with his brothers, and in my mind, this combined cake, lovingly prepared by our dad, speaks volumes about our unity as a family.

Johnny was about four or so years old when we took a trip. If you've ever been on a long trip with a large family, you know that Mom and Dad have their hands full, especially when the youngest is still a baby. As his big sister, I took on the task of helping care for Johnny as much as I could; this helped form a special bond between the two of us. Looking back, this trip also showed me how family and love are the road map of the future.

Johnny loved James Brown so much growing up that my little brother began impersonating the entertainer by the time he was six. On the sidewalk in front of our home,

Johnny did what no other kid in the hood could do: He did splits, slides, spins, and much more. He didn't mind in the least that his performances drew a crowd.

Finally, brethren, whatsoever things are true, whatsoever things are honest, whatsoever things are just, whatsoever things are pure, whatsoever things are lovely, whatsoever things are of good report; if there be any virtue, and if there be any praise, think on these things.
—Philippians 4:8

He was strong and gentle all at once. He could pin me in a headlock I couldn't escape from when we played wrestle, and he sneak-attacked Mama with hugs and kisses. It makes me smile just thinking about the way Mama laughed when he caught her by surprise, and then she'd say, "Okay, Bunny, that's enough now."

Like all of us, Johnny inherited a love of food, which for him turned into a love for cooking. After moving out, he started to barbecue mutton. He cooked this after he vowed not to eat pork again. We didn't know what mutton was, so he decided to give us an opportunity to taste it. Johnny hosted a barbecue to showcase his masterpiece. Not long after, he became known as the Englewood barbecue.

Johnny grew up to be a simple man. He's there when you need him, and he doesn't put much stock in holidays. He thinks that every day is a holiday, and ought to be celebrated as such.

Johnny married a beautiful woman named Cherise, has two stepdaughters, and is now a grandfather. He lives in

California, where he's known as "Johnny Do Every-thang."

Lessons Learned

Growing up with my six siblings has taught me so much about the importance of family values like loyalty, duty, and respect. There are many precious memories of us playing together, traveling together, cooking together, eating together, and working together, all while shaping each other and helping each other to learn and grow. My siblings and I have learned how to resolve conflicts and forgive each other. We have learned the importance of unity and sticking together, loving each other uncondi-tionally. This influence has affected how I love my own family, and for that I am grateful every day.

WORKBOOK

Chapter Four Reflection

Read Mark 12:31.

Your family is your first opportunity to learn to love and consider others.

Louise was blessed with many siblings, each of whom helped to shape her own life.

How did the size and birth order of your family affect your personality and direction in life? What desires do you have for your own children's relationships with each other, and how can you help them to grow and remain close?

_____

_____

_____

_____

_____

CHAPTER FIVE

My High-School Years

Trust in the LORD with all thine heart; and lean not unto thine own understanding. In all thy ways acknowledge him and he shall direct thy path.
—Proverbs 3:5–6

Be still, and know that I am God: I will be exalted among the heathen, I will be exalted in the earth.
—Psalm 46:10

I told Mama I wanted to attend high school in a different neighborhood district. She talked to Daddy, and they enrolled me in Simeon Vocational High, located in the Chatham area or South Chicago. I took two different buses to get to school each day.

I found out later that Boo and I were under the same roof for one semester during my freshman year, but neither one of us was aware of it. His family couldn't afford the bus fare to get him to and from school, so he walked the distance. The extremes of Chicago weather eventually got the best of him, and he had to go to the neighborhood school after that.

Before I knew it, it was my senior year. It was an exciting time in my life, and I was looking forward to my senior luncheon, to prom, and to the spring picnics.

I didn't have a date to take me to the prom, but I wasn't feeling too bad because a lot of students were going solo or in groups. Two weeks before the big dance, we had a luncheon. I was sitting at the table in the banquet hall straight across from the star of the school baseball team. I'd never given him any of my time, but that day I noticed him sitting there, checking me out. Out of the blue, he asked me to be his date to prom.

We'd had no conversation prior to that, and I was caught off guard. Everyone at the table was watching, waiting for my answer, so I had to think fast. I said, "Yes. I'll be your date." My attitude about the dance suddenly completely changed. I was too excited to wait for the bus, so I walked home to share the news with Mama and my family. I had a date to my senior prom!

I didn't have much to spend on my prom dress, but Mama and I made an event of it. Somehow blue became my color that year. When I look at pictures, my graduation dress is blue, the outfit I wore to the luncheon was blue, and so was my prom dress. Like most girls, I dreamed of the fun that night would be.

As with many things, the dream and the reality were quite different. While I had a date to accompany me, several of my friends did not. I felt pulled in two different directions. I wanted to spend time with my date, but I also wanted to be with my friends, whom I knew better.

Added to that, my date had driven a friend and his date with us to the prom. She wasn't enjoying herself, so she wanted to leave before the prom was over and be taken home, which was a bit of a drive.

I was disappointed at having to leave so early, but I have the feeling Daddy was secretly relieved when I returned home before the curfew he'd set. Unfortunately, I never mentioned that there would be a senior picnic at Great America the following day, so I didn't have permission to go from Daddy. I'm not sure why I didn't ask Daddy about it; I guess I was afraid it'd be asking too much to participate in two events like that back to back.

So, when my date called the next day to arrange to pick me up, I had to find a way to tell him I couldn't go. I spent the entire day thinking about how much fun everyone was having on the water slides, roller coasters, and other activities. I wished I had asked Daddy; maybe he would have let me go if I had.

My date called me later that day to see if he could come over and see me. When he got to our house, he told me how much fun my classmates had had and how he had missed my presence. We hung out for a while and then went for a drive in his neon-blue Cougar. As time went on, we became an item, and we started doing everything together.

One Saturday morning, while I was visiting with his family and talking to his older sister about her job working for a radio station, an older woman burst into the house. She'd spotted my boyfriend and me getting out of the car and entering the house together. I remember she was wearing a large T-shirt with the words UNDER

CONSTRUCTION on it and an arrow pointing down at her large stomach.

She was cursing and screaming, demanding to know who I was. She told me she was expecting my boyfriend's baby and that he had to take care of her and their child.

His mother had to get involved to calm this angry woman down, and I remember wondering what the heck was going on. We continued to date for about nine months after that incident. He worked while he attended school to become a paramedic, and I started college. Then his child was born, our schedules went haywire, and I was not very comfortable with the baby mama drama, so we ended our relationship.

I thank God for my mother. She was my anchor during this time, and she knew just what to say after the breakup. I was in a bad place and needed the love and support of my mama to bring me out of it. I dated off and on after that, but I never got involved in anything serious. I couldn't see myself giving my heart to anyone ever again. With my first love, I had been carefree and open; after him, I kept a wall around my heart, so I wouldn't be hurt by someone again.

My Angel Returns

A few years later, I attended the funeral of a former classmate of mine. She and her brother had both died, and the siblings' funeral services were held together. So many people attended the wake that there wasn't enough room for everyone to enter the church. People were covering the sidewalk and the street; police were on crowd control. I had never seen anything like it in my life. This was the first funeral I had attended as a young adult, without my family members being present with me.

It was impossible to get through the crowd, and as I tried to work my way through the sea of people, I spotted Boo also working his way into the church. I shouted from a distance, but he was moving so quickly and was so focused and determined to get inside, he never heard me.

I didn't see Boo again until the spring talent show. Sarah Ruth wanted to participate, so we all went together. And there was John—tall, dark chocolate, and as handsome as ever, with guitar in his hand and cowboy hat on his head, wowing the audience with his performance.

Sarah Ruth was hollering the whole time, "That's him! That's him, Lou."

During his performance, Boo threw his cowboy hat into the audience. The girls near the stage went crazy trying to catch it.

My sister and I took our time walking home that night, laughing and talking about Boo's performance the entire way. The evening was so pleasant, and it was rare for us to be out alone that late in the evening. We tried to capture every moment along the way—from the feel of the breeze to the scent of the spring blossoms.

The next day, there was talk all over the neighborhood about that talent show. I was glad to have been there to see it firsthand.

Not long after the spring talent show, I heard that John had left Chicago to join the Job Corps and the U.S. Navy. I saw his father, Reverend Elijah Buckner, one Sunday after church, and he told me that I was going to be his daughter-in-law one day. Before I knew what I was doing, I'd play-punched him in the belly.

He started holding his stomach and laughing uncontrollably. I asked him what was so funny, and he said it was true, that I was going to be his daughter-in-law. I walked away thinking, *This man is crazy.*

I told my sister what Reverend Buckner had said when I got home, and she laughed and laughed. Turns out the reverend just knew before I did. Not long after his revelation, I received my first love letter from John. I had no idea he even had access to my address. I was flattered when I received the first letter and several more that followed.

John was living in Louisiana when he received word that his father had passed in his sleep at the family home in Englewood. He called me soon after he arrived back in town. I could hear lots of people in the background doing their best to console his family.

I remember it being late. He asked me to come over and be with him at the house. I didn't know what to do to ease his pain, or what to say. I decided it wasn't the best time to show up, but we stayed on the phone for little while longer. He talked, and I mostly just listened. He was grateful for that. Before we hung up, I told him I'd talk to him the next day.

John decided to stay in after the funeral, so he could take care of his mother. I thought it was a good thing for both of them. They needed each other to help ease their grief.

More than Friendship

Later that year, my girlfriend Tracie wanted to have a birthday party, but she didn't have a place to hold it. I had a friend with an apartment, so we ran the idea by him about holding the party there.

I decided as soon as we started planning the party that I was going to invite John. I called his mother's house repeatedly, hoping to catch him and invite him, but he was never home. Later, I found out that John had been working evenings. When I finally reached John, my face was all smiles the second I heard his voice. I could tell by his voice he was surprised and very pleased to hear my voice, too. We talked for a little while before I finally invited him to the party. He agreed to come, and I told him I was looking forward to seeing him.

Tracie's birthday was the first time I'd hosted a party of any kind. I felt so grown-up as I prepared the fried chicken, potato salad, tuna salad, and several dips with chips.

It seemed like forever before John arrived at the party. I remember he had on a cream and gold button-down dress shirt, a burgundy vest with a blazer of the same color, and tan pants. My heart started to race as he stood back, looking around the room. All of a sudden, I felt shy and speechless, but after I regained my composure, I approached him.

At six-foot-two, John towered over me. I looked up at him and into his eyes, and he looked into mine. At that point, I was selfish with my special guest. I didn't want to leave his side, although I had other friends in the same room whom I should have been paying attention to, as well. John wasn't able to stay long, but my heart was full when he left.

Overall, the party was a success. Tracie was happy. The guests were happy. And I was happy.

About a week or so later, Tracie and I met up again to spend an afternoon together at the mall and listen to some new records. I checked in with Mama as evening approached, and she told me that John had called. He was going to be at my house around eight that night. I didn't waste a minute. I got a taxi and rushed straight home and up to my room to freshen up.

When I came downstairs, John was waiting for me. The first thing he did was ask for a glass of water. He drank it as if he hadn't had anything to drink in quite a while. We sat on Mama's blue sectional sofa with the thick hard plastic that squeaked when you moved and stuck to you when you got up.

It was a short visit, but he continued to come around after that night. Tracie played a big role in me deciding to date John. After a bit, he began to call me "cute in the face, slim in the waist."

He was working downtown as the manager of the health club in the hotel. Because of his position, the hotel restaurant was available to John. I'd meet him there for dinner once a week, sometimes with Tracie.

I got to know his mother around this time and started helping her care for her personal needs when her health started failing. Mrs. Buckner was a woman who didn't hold back her thoughts. Because of that, there were a number of people who thought she was mean. I think part of the reason for her bluntness was that she grew up as foster child. That might have been why she was always protecting her well-being on so many levels. I simply saw her as a woman who wanted the best for her children, just like my parents wanted the best for me and my siblings.

After a while, it was decided that John's mother needed more care. John's family decided it was best if she moved down to Baton Rouge, where her daughters lived with their husbands and families. This way, John's mother could receive all the support she needed.

By the time she moved away, I had become very comfortable with Mrs. Buckner, and I had the feeling she wouldn't mind me as a daughter-in-law someday. I was also getting to know John's siblings, having met all of John's two sisters and five brothers in one setting or another.

The Proposal

In December of that year, John invited me to a musical celebrating the anniversary of the church he was attending. The program was at four in the afternoon and just a few blocks from my home, so we walked together, hand in hand.

The church was also the pastor's family's residence, so the pastor made small talk with us before the program. Then, we made our way to the sanctuary.

For some reason, I was starting to feel uncomfortable. There were lots of young women my age looking in my direction, whispering, and talking among themselves. I took a seat and didn't move. The program got underway, and at the end, John spoke. While speaking, he said, "I want to introduce my fiancée."

I couldn't believe what I was hearing. I was furious, wondering why he had brought me out here to embarrass me. And I wanted to know who this woman was to whom he was engaged.

His announcement didn't just get a reaction out of me, but the entire congregation was talking at once. That's when he asked me to stand and he introduced me by name. He asked me to marry him right there in front of the entire congregation.

I froze. I hadn't been expecting the question any more than the congregation had. I don't know what he was feeling while I stood there, but once I regained my voice, I said yes, agreeing to be his wife.

Saying yes was easy compared to what waited for us next. I was nothing but nerves the whole walk home. I wasn't sure what to expect from my parents upon hearing the news.

Daddy was already in bed, so Mama had to wake him up. He came out of my parents' room with a half-smile on his face, as though he knew why we were there.

John and I sat with Mama and Daddy at the dining room table. We were incredibly nervous, while my parents gave each other a secret look that only they could understand.

John told Daddy he loved me with all his heart and asked for his permission for us to marry. Daddy counseled us for over two hours about what marriage was about, a man's responsibilities to his wife, and the duties of a wife to a husband.

I remember him saying we were going to have some black children, because we both had dark skin. When I was growing up, Daddy had always said the blacker the berry, the sweeter the juice, so I saw no problem with his statement. He went on to say, "Think of the babies when picking a mate; good-looking people make good-looking children." He also reminded us that love doesn't pay bills; work and money do.

Daddy talked and talked about his and Mama's early days when they married and shared the financial advice they'd been given by their first realtor.

I didn't sleep much that night after John left. When I woke up the next morning, I went straight to Mama's room. She was curious and had a lot of questions. She'd been pretty quiet at the table, listening while Daddy talked to us.

She was happy for me and John. I told her how John had proposed to me, how I felt about it, and so on. We laughed and talked most of that morning.

Later that day, John called me to see if we could get together. We met each other halfway, because John only lived a few blocks away from my house. As we approached each other, John opened his arms, I fell into his body, and he closed me in. We were both all smiles as we began to make plans for our wedding day.

We decided to get married after a year. We both wanted a big wedding, so we wanted the time to save up and get everything together. We had to consider wedding rings, the church, reception expenses, and of course, more money to get us started in our new life together, of which he had little at the time.

John and I went to pick out rings together on Sixty-Third and Halsted, at one of the well-known jewelers in the area. I used to stop outside the window and look at the diamonds sparkle every time I passed by. This time, I was skipping the window and entering the door.

Most of the rings were too expensive for our budget, but we were determined to purchase our rings that day from this jeweler. We wanted to show our expression of love for each other to the world. We finally decided on a beautiful set, with John getting a matching wedding band.

Because we didn't have much in our savings yet, John opened an account at the jewelry store. A few days later, when the rings were ready, we returned to the store to pick them up. John placed my engagement ring on my finger and sealed it with a warm and tender kiss. We were floating on cloud nine and never wanted to come back down.

Chapter Five Reflection

Read Romans 8:28–29.

Often when God says "no" to your desires or plans, He gives something better in His timing.

Louise was brokenhearted after things did not work out between her and her high school sweetheart, but God had other, better plans for her.

Reflect on a time when a broken heart or a major disappointment was really God's protection and kindness to you. How can you use that experience to shape how you approach heartache in the future?

_____

_____

_____

_____

_____

CHAPTER SIX

Making It, No Matter What

We hit our first roadblock a few months after John and I got engaged. The details surrounding the event don't matter as much as the result of the fallout. John was trying to help with a situation, but he didn't know all the details. There was a fight, and the next thing we knew, Daddy had banned him from our house.

Our marriage plans fell behind because of the tension with my family. John and I occasionally met in the pouring rain between our homes, his arms wrapped around me as we spoke. Sometimes we met at the park. Other times, we saw each other at his house or at a restaurant. Not long after the year-mark of our engagement, I started feeling sick and suspected that I was pregnant. I was afraid of what my parents would say, especially my father. I told John that I might be expecting a baby, our love child. He was excited about being a father, but very concerned about me because of the situation.

He was by my side when I took the pregnancy test at

Cook County Hospital. Afterward, we got a bite to eat and took a walk outside while waiting on the test results. I was nervous, and by this time, John was talking to me, trying to reassure me that everything was going to be all right with us. After a while, we made it back to the hospital waiting area to learn the results.

I was pregnant.

John held me as we traveled back home on the EL train. I stayed quiet most of the way. He walked me to the door and gave me a hug and kiss, but because of my father's edict, he could go no farther. I told him I would call him later.

Mama was in the kitchen cooking like she always was at that time of day. I remembered the time I had asked Mama for another sister when I was little, as well as her response. I walked in and said "Mama, I am going to have a baby."

Mama immediately poured me a glass of milk and told me to sit down. She seemed happy. She said I would need a lot of milk during my pregnancy.

It took me another week to break the news to Daddy. I didn't want there to be further hard feelings between him and John, and I agonized every day about how to tell him the truth.

I finally told my father I had to talk to him. He sat down with me, and I wondered if he already knew what I was going to tell him. If that was the case, he was playing it cool, which he was good at doing, until the time was right, and he played his hand.

"Daddy, I am going to have a baby," I said. I couldn't believe it when he looked at me and responded, "Yeah, I could look at your neck and tell it had changed. Your heartbeat is much faster."

He asked what John and I were are going to do. I said we were still going to be married and we would raise our child together. All during the pregnancy, John was not allowed to visit me at the house, so I still had to leave to see him.

Days and weeks went by, along with visits to the clinic for prenatal care. John accompanied me whenever possible. Months later, he started shopping nonstop for our baby. This daddy-to-be was on it.

He had friends drop off baby supplies at the house while he waited at the car: the baby bed, mattress, changing table, tons of diapers—everything a baby needed and then some.

My brother Joseph assisted with bringing things into the house, up the stairs, and setting them up in the room for the arrival of our new baby. This was before my baby shower. I had gotten so large with my pregnancy I looked as if I was having twins or more.

Toward the end of my pregnancy, one day when I was getting ready for church, Daddy looked at me and said, "Lou, I think you better stay home."

He chuckled and said that I was just too large and at risk of having the baby while I was out.

The baby's due date was closing in, and I was still flipping pages, looking for that perfect girl name. I had the middle name picked out. I got it from watching *Little House on the Prairie* years before my pregnancy.

This baby would be the first grandchild in my family, and everyone was excited. They all had some suggestions for what the name of the baby should be; John Junior or Little Louise were not options. John and I both finally settled on LaKeshia Melissa Buckner.

With the ongoing tension between my father and my love, I had to make many difficult decisions as a young woman and a daughter. First Corinthians 13:4–8a came to mind often:

> *Charity suffereth long, and is kind; charity envieth not; charity vaunteth not itself, is not puffed up, doth not behave itself unseemly, seeketh not her own, is not easily provoked, thinketh no evil; rejoiceth not in iniquity, but rejoiceth in the truth; beareth all things, believeth all things, hopeth all things, endureth all things. Charity never faileth.*

The three characteristics of love that stood out to me most from these verses were that love is kind, love is gentle, and love is forgiving. I knew that I must exhibit all three. I cried many times, hoping for peace and comfort for all involved. I loved my father and I loved John. I asked myself why I was going through this turmoil when this should be such a happy time in my life. I was in love and carrying my fiancé's child. God had sent me the man of my dreams in the dead of winter, but it felt like springtime, like all things were blooming.

I reminded myself that God knew what was happening in my life, and that He was there with me in the middle of my confusion and pain.

They say that what doesn't kill you makes you stronger. Well, that trial didn't kill me. I'm still here.

Mama stayed with me at the hospital for a while after I went into labor. Back then, fathers weren't allowed in the delivery room, so John couldn't be there to hold my hand. He sent me love notes instead, each delivered by the nurse. After LaKeshia was born, I was taken to a semi-private room where another love letter was waiting for me, along with an *Essence* magazine.

> *When thou passest through the waters, I will be with thee; and through the rivers, they shall not overflow thee: when thou walkest through the fire, thou shalt not beburned; neither shall the flame kindle upon thee.*
> **—Isaiah 43:2**

Things between Daddy and John didn't improve after LaKeshia's birth. Boo and I were still engaged, but I was unable to defy my father and marry the man with whom I wanted to spend my life. Darnell Westly Buckner was born about a year later. By the time Darnell entered the world, I'd moved in with my first cousin for a brief time and then back in with my parents.

John and I talked on the phone at night and listened to "The Closer I Get to You" by Roberta Flack and Donny Hathaway. Neither of us was in a place financially to be able to take care of ourselves, and I had Daddy in my ear the whole time. I was afraid and confused, and I felt like I was going to lose my mind.

However, John was constant, and we were determined to figure out a way to make things work and to begin our lives together as husband and wife. We became diligent in putting money aside, just like Daddy had told me and my siblings to do when we were young. Make a little. Save a little.

In time, we had fifteen hundred dollars in cash stashed away in my top dresser drawer. At that point in time, setting aside that amount of money was no easy thing.

We set February 14 as our wedding day. It was John's idea. But when that day came, I chickened out. I can only imagine the hurt I truly caused him. But exactly a month later, on March 14, after a long conversation the night before, we decided together it was time.

The only person in my family I told that I was getting married that day was my sister Sarah Ruth. She was getting ready for work and wished me luck before leaving. I got my babies up, fed, and dressed before getting myself ready. I didn't have a dress, just a blue sweater and jeans. But as I waited for the taxi to arrive, I couldn't help but think, *Today I will start a new journey, trusting God and my husband-to-be.*

Our Wedding Day at Last

Boo wasn't home when we arrived at his family's house. His family said he'd run out on an errand. So, I waited with my two babies in the living room. I wondered if John had decided not to marry me this time.

It seemed like forever that I sat in the living room, while the rest of John's family was in the kitchen. I guess, in reality it was about thirty minutes before he got back. He came rushing in the door with a dry-cleaning plastic bag, saying, "Hey, y'all, I will be right back. I'm going up to get ready."

With that, he was up the stairs to the second floor of the house. All I could do was breathe a sigh of tremendous relief and say a brief prayer of thanks.

John's wedding garb matched mine: a blue sweater and blue jeans. In the end, love isn't what you wear—it's what's inside your heart.

It was windy and rainy outside, the usual for March. I got the babies dressed in their coats and hats, and all of a sudden, the area around the front door got crowded.

His auntie and two cousins were coming along with us to witness the wedding. We were married at Pleasant Gift Missionary Baptist Church by John's uncle, Reverend Robert L. Buckner. John had a cousin who was doing janitorial work there, getting the church ready for Sunday service. John told him to put his mop down and be his best man.

We were all smiles as Uncle Robert signed the marriage license. Our wedding banquet was inside of a Walgreens drugstore. We got high chairs for both babies and ordered our food, John feeding one baby while I fed the other.

At the end of the night, I went back home to my parents. I didn't say a word to anyone else about my wedding. We continued to live apart for another month, still keeping our marriage secret from my parents while looking frantically for an apartment to rent.

During the same time, my older brother and his wife and family were moving out of their nice apartment. It was a godsend. Solo put us in touch with the landlord, and we were able to schedule an appointment with him.

I remember when we got the news that the apartment

was ours. We took a taxi over to the building right away. The landlord was to meet us there around four. The landlord was looking out of the first-floor window when we arrived.

We were greeted and entered the well-kept courtyard. The first-floor unit door was open. John paid the rent money and the landlord gave us the lease and keys and left.

We had nothing but the built-in Murphy bed and some furniture my brother and his wife had left behind for that first night. Boo got a truck the next day, and, with the help of my younger brother, he moved our belongings out of my parents' house from the rear at the alley. John still abided my daddy's decree, and he didn't set a foot in my parents' home.

Daddy called me about two weeks later. He'd been told by someone from our church that John and I had gotten married. I thought about what I'd done and waited for Daddy to let loose on me. However, the explosion never came. Before he got off the phone, he told me to come by the house to get my wedding gift.

That weekend, I made the trip over to the house, trying to think positive thoughts along the way. I rang the doorbell and then used my key to get in.

There was Daddy, sitting in the dining room at the head of the table facing the entrance door, as he had done forever. I thought back to our conversation around this table a few years back, but this time John wasn't with me. We made some small talk and he gifted me with five hundred dollars, the same gift he gave to each of my siblings when they married. Things remained icy between my daddy and my husband, but I always look back at that gift fondly. It reminds me that when things are hard, we can still reach across the breach, and that no matter what happens, family remains family.

No Job, but Still a Breadwinner

Not long after my visit with Daddy, John was laid off from his job. That's a difficult place for any husband to find himself in. We had two small children to care for, rent to pay, and I was a stay-at-home wife and mother.

John didn't forget about his responsibility of being a husband and father, providing for his family. With no job in reach, he took to the alleys, going through garbage cans picking up aluminum cans and scrap metal. He had a metal shopping cart he filled and pushed to the scrapyards. This went on for five long years, Monday through Saturday, from five in the morning to eight at night.

My angel never worked on Sunday. That day was dedicated to the Lord, and he used his musical talents to play guitar at church.

I did my best to make our home a haven. I taught my two children their colors, letters, and numbers before they left for kindergarten. At night, we read Dr. Seuss, a children's Bible, and the Golden Books before I tucked the kids into bed.

When John got home, I had a warm bath ready and food waiting. He worked hard, and he was tired and dirty when he got home at night. I wanted him to feel like a king and to be able to rest from his struggles.

During this time, John applied with the city to become

a firefighter. He studied and took strenuous physical exams, but he never heard back from them. We learned later that there was a class action lawsuit filed on behalf of the black applicants who had been passed over because of their race.

In the meantime, John kept doing what he could to provide for his family. Yes, life was harder than we'd have liked it to be, but our love was stronger than the hardship we experienced. We knew we'd get through this difficult time together.

Our staples consisted of a five-pound bag of chicken wings and five pounds of white potatoes most weeks. We added a two-liter bottle of Pepsi or Coca-Cola when we could. I tried to mix up how I cooked the chicken and potatoes. Sometimes I fried them. Sometimes I baked the chicken and mashed the potatoes. It wasn't much, but it kept our bellies filled.

John and I were both smokers at the time, as were many of the people of our generation. But we tried to limit ourselves and the money we spent on cigarettes. One day we would buy the filtered brand I liked; another day we got his choice of smokes.

I have fond memories of walking our kids up the street to the local park in the evenings, and then sitting on the stoop outside our back door when we returned. John and I used that time to thank God for each other, for our family, and for our love.

Once LaKeshia and Darnell were old enough to go to school, I found work filling temporary positions in downtown Chicago. Finances became less tight, so we could afford more of the things that we wanted. We even began entertaining friends and family in our home.

Oprah had just come on the scene, so, for fun, I created my own talk show, called *Talking with Lou*. I would interview our guests when they came to visit, and we all had a lot fun talking and laughing together.

One Christmas, the kids, Keshia and D, got an Atari 2600, which was a big-ticket item back then in the early 1980s. Their first game was Pole Position, a race car game that was one of the most popular games at the time it was released.

We had it set up in the living room on the television, and it captured the attention of everyone who arrived for dinner. It wasn't long before the adults took over the game and the kids retreated to their rooms.

We should have been ashamed, but we were having too much fun competing with each other. We played the game into the wee hours of the next morning, and several of our guests crashed out wherever we could find space for them.

I served Christmas dinner leftovers for breakfast the next morning, and we continued to play that game throughout the day. I remember that Christmas fondly—even if the kids don't.

Family Truce

It was about this time that Mama and Daddy started coming around to visit from time to time.

Daddy had bought a couple of buildings that needed some paint on the outside, but all my brothers were afraid of heights. Being up high didn't bother John, so Daddy asked him if he'd putty and paint all the windows on the second and third floors.

Daddy told him, "I can't pay you, but I can feed you." So, after John had worked, he got to enjoy some of my Mama's home cooking.

Working for Daddy gave John the tools and skills he needed to make painting and plastering his side hustle. He took on projects that others wouldn't. I was amazed watching John take on some of the jobs he did.

John's big brother Robert was a career Chicago police officer for the CPD. He always said he admired my husband because John did things he didn't think he could do to take care of his family. When a position opened in Robert's office, he told John about it. John applied and was hired.

After fifteen years of marriage and working odd jobs here and there wherever we could find them, we were finally approaching a place in life where we could begin dreaming of being homeowners.

We took the advice Daddy had given us when we first told him we planned to marry. We bought only what was needed to live: food, gas for the car to go to church and occasionally visit my family, and clothes and shoes. Everything else we earned went into savings. We found a real estate agent, gathered our references, and secured a loan, and then, once we had everything in place, it was time to go house hunting.

WORKBOOK

Chapter Six Reflection

Read 1 Corinthians 13:4–7.

Genuine love overcomes the greatest of obstacles.

Louise and John faced numerous challenges throughout the early days of their relationship.

Describe a time in your own life when love overcame great hardships.

_____

_____

_____

_____

_____

_____

_____

_____

CHAPTER SEVEN

My Storyteller

Many of the old stories begin with, "Once upon a time…"

Our marriage was no different. After long days of struggling to make ends meet and make sure our children's needs were met, we lay together in bed.

John pulled me close and wrapped his arms around me, and I laid my head on his chest. He asked, "Are you good and comfortable, baby?"

I answered, "Yes baby."

That signaled for him to start telling his bedtime story to me. It was a long story that involved mystery and romance, and he continued until my restlessness turned to rest.

There were nights when he fell asleep before me and I lay there watching the ceiling and listening to him breathe. Even that sound was soothing. He always asked how I slept when we woke up in the morning. On the days I hesitated, he said, "Baby, you should have woken me."

I told him that wasn't right, that he needed his sleep, too. He replied, "It's no bother. I want you to be happy and rested."

On stormy nights, when the thunder was roaring, heavy rains were pouring down, and lightning was flashing, my angel held me in his safe arms until the storm was over.

I took pride in the gentleness of this man. I appreciated him putting me first, morning and night. And these bedtime traditions have given me many happy memories. Over the years, my angel told a good many different stories. Some were fiction, some were based on the truth, and some were comical, but each was told to bring me joy.

John has always had an interest in Native American history. He placed a few dreamcatchers on our headboard, which is a tradition in some tribes.

The idea is that happy, optimistic dreams will pass through the net, while the negative dreams or nightmares will become ensnared. Some believe negative dreams pass through the center of the catcher, while the good dreams are trapped. Those good dreams go on to become a part of the dreamer's destiny.

And that's what my angel wanted for us—a happy future, full of good dreams.

Chapter Seven Reflection

Read Proverbs 5:18.

Enjoy life with your spouse, and work to bring them joy, too!

John worked hard and used his gifts to make Louise's life as easy and pleasant as he could.

How can you use your talents, abilities, and gifts to bring joy to your spouse or others?

_____

_____

_____

_____

_____

_____

_____

CHAPTER EIGHT

Our Children

Children's children are the crown of old men; and the glory of children are their fathers.
—Proverbs 17:6

Our children were raised in the church and learned the importance of reading God's Word from a young age. John and I believed in bringing up our children in the way they should go, so that, as adults, they wouldn't depart from God (Proverbs 22:6).

My Black Diamond

Our beautiful firstborn daughter, LaKeshia (Keshia) Melissa Buckner, is a very ambitious and headstrong child. Like her father, she's always moving and never settling for the present situation. Her father calls her Ke-Ke. I call her Black Diamond and Keshia Weshia (among a few other pet names).

When she was about three years old, a young married

couple moved into our apartment building. We chatted whenever we saw each other, but I wouldn't say we were good friends.

One morning, our neighbor stepped outside to check her mail. She had something cooking on the stove and her baby was asleep in the crib. Somehow, the door closed behind her and locked her out.

She came banging on my door in a panic. Being a mother, I knew exactly what she was feeling. We had to get her inside and make sure her baby was okay. I had an idea, but if it was going to work, I'd need Keshia's help.

I dressed her in her pink snowsuit, her winter hat, mittens, and snow boots, making sure she was covered head to toe. The back doors of our apartments had four small window panes, too small for anyone except Keshia to fit through.

I broke the glass and cleared away all the shards before turning to my little hero. I told her I needed her to crawl through the window and go straight to the front door and grab the key from the lock. Then she needed to come right back to me and give me the key. Once she understood she was helping to keep a little girl safe, she was all too happy to be Mommy's helper.

After Keshia brought me the key and we got the door open, I gave her the biggest hug and kiss. My neighbor ran straight to her baby, who had slept through the whole ordeal.

As a child, Keshia squeezed between me and her father, and sat in the middle of us all time. John said, "Just wait until you get a boyfriend. I'm going to pay you back. Big-time." She laughed and said, "Daddy, Daddy, you are not going to do that."

He responded, "Hell if I ain't."

When she was old enough, Keshia sang in the church choir, just like her mama and grandmama before her. She was thirteen when she committed her life to Christ and was baptized.

Keshia's love to travel was clear from the day she got her first driver's license. She was thrilled by the prospect of freedom and has been a traveler ever since. She loves to drive, and if she can't go somewhere by car, she goes by plane.

Keshia is a very caring, no-nonsense individual. She refuses to accept an "it can't be done" mindset. Family and sisterhood are very dear to her heart and soul. She trusts God for who He is in her life.

LaKeshia became more focused after becoming a member of the Order of the Eastern Star, a branch of the Masons that is open to female relatives of Masons. She spends a lot of time working with different charities and fellowships within the Order. She's a leader and an advocate for women who have experienced or survived domestic violence. She is a prime example of sisterhood.

She's made a career for herself as an event planner. She's learned under celebrity wedding planners and events planners from around the country, studying the business inside and out. I've watched her go from planning her own wedding to working with park districts and small chapels and on to world-class venues and prominent venues. She shares her grandmama's love of fashion and is always keeping up with the latest trends. Like her daddy and her brother, she's also a bit of a workaholic.

Keshia's seen her share of turmoil and adversity throughout the years, but she continues to be a fierce human being. She's taken on the role of a single parent to her two amazing sons, teaching them self-value, self-motivation, and persistence. If there's one thing she's learned, it's to count it all joy.

My Son

> *My son, forget not my law; but let thine heart keep my commandments: for length of days, and long life, and peace, shall they add to thee.*
> **—Proverbs 3:1–2**

Our son, Darnell Westly Buckner, is called D most of the time. My mother nicknamed him Chip because he was so little at birth.

Because he and Keshia were so close in age, it sometimes seemed like I was raising twins. When I was a kid, I'd dreamed of having twins, one boy and one girl, one pregnancy, and then done. I didn't understand then how busy two babies would keep me. Diapers, formula, teething, talking, bath time, bedtime, and walking—it was all one big event.

D was a reserved child, but he was smart. God also used him to protect us one night when he was around seven years old.

We'd all gone to bed for the night, but John had gotten hungry and put one of his smoked sausages in a pot to boil. However, he fell asleep while the pot was still on the stove. My and John's bedroom was nearest to the kitchen and began to fill with smoke, but we didn't notice. It was D who woke me with his little voice, "There's smoke, Mama. There's smoke."

It took us a minute to realize what was happening. Once my foggy brain woke up, I jumped up out of the bed and shook John. Then I ran to the kitchen to turn off the pot.

We had to open all the windows to air the smoke out, but the kids' room had no smoke smell at all. The air was clear and fresh.

I thank God to this day for using my little boy to save us from what could have been a tragedy.

Many of Darnell's classmates grew up without a father in their home or life. He always felt that was unfortunate, and it made a lasting impact on the path he chose for his life.

He loved baseball and tennis, and he served as a junior usher in the church. Like his sister, he dedicated his life to God around the age of 13.

He tested above average on all his tests, including the SAT and ACT, but he let his smarts go to his head.

He was a good kid for the most part. There was one time, though, when he started acting out toward me. This went on for about a week, before I finally had had enough. I told his daddy he needed to check his son, because I didn't like him, and he didn't like me, either. John sat him down and they had a long talk about how things would be in our home. After that, it was like I had a new son.

D has become a self-made entrepreneur, organizer, and promoter. He's made it his mission to spearhead change for the underprivileged youth in our community. He's very confident and speaks what others dare not say. Young people look up to him like they would to a father or big brother. Too many young men and women have no father in their lives, so Darnell does what he can to show these young men and women how to become their best selves.

Darnell married his beautiful wife, Thaneshia, and they have three children. I often commend his wife on how great she is as a mother to my grandchildren. It is a blessing.

> *And when all things shall be subdued unto him, then shall the Son also himself be subject unto him that put all things under him, that God may be all in all.*
> *—1 Corinthians 15:28*

Darnell has had some bumps and bruises along the way, but he never wavers. He keeps pressing forward, with the promises of God pressed close to his heart. He's had the opportunity to work with some prominent figures, but his greatest concern is for the children—our future. His desire to build up young people drives him to speak out for our community. Darnell believes in a future when Christ is going to return in power and triumph over all His enemies, including death itself.

Being a mother hasn't always been easy, but my children are two of the best gifts God has ever given me. It is a delight to watch them succeed as adults and flourish in the ways of the Lord.

Chapter Eight Reflection

Read James 1:27.

Protecting and helping the fatherless shows your love for God.

Darnell felt burdened for his classmates who grew up without a father, and as an adult, he stepped in to be a father figure to those who needed that example.

In what ways are you showing your love for God by caring for the fatherless? How can you reflect the nature of the Heavenly Father to young people who do not know what it means to have their own father?

_____

_____

_____

_____

_____

CHAPTER NINE

Our Dream House

For this man [Jesus] was counted worthy of more glory than Moses, inasmuch as he who hath builded the house hath more honour than the house.

For every house is builded by some man; but he that built all things is God.
—Hebrews 3:3–4

We found a few nice houses for sale during our search, but most of the ones that were within our budget were in deplorable condition. We kept looking, not willing to settle for a home that wouldn't be a good fit for our family.

I was amazed at the difference in what some would consider to be "nice" or "livable." There were several properties that we just did a drive-by on. We didn't even bother stopping to get out of the car.

John and I kept pressing on, looking for the house that spoke to us. We wanted something bright with God's sunlight: inviting, warm, and cozy. Like everyone, we wanted a home that reflected who we were.

One early evening in the middle of the year, we were out with our agent to look at three different properties. We'd barely pulled up to the second house before John started shouting, "This is it. This is our house!"

I wasn't convinced so quickly. However, once we were inside, I started warming up to the possibility. The house was all brick with a stone front. There were nice picture windows to let in plenty of natural light. It had three full bathrooms, five bedrooms, a rear sun porch, a finished basement, plenty of yard space with a patio in the back, and a two-and-a-half-car garage.

The owners were asking for a little more than what our budget allowed for, but we made an offer that was accepted. My father's longtime attorney was notified to help close the deal, and he informed us that we'd need a home inspection before making this huge purchase. Fortunately, he knew just the man for the job.

John and D were at the house for over eight hours on the day of the inspection. The inspector crawled all over every square inch of the house, checking the roof, foundation, plumbing, electricity—you name it.

While they were there, baby girl and I were at home, waiting anxiously for word on how the inspection had gone. We didn't have cell phones in those days, so John couldn't update me on the progress throughout the day. I had to wait until he got home to learn that the inspector had done a very thorough job.

A few more days passed before our attorney presented us with the final inspection report. The house had passed with flying colors. If we still wanted the house, it was a go.

The days that followed were filled with excitement and anticipation. Mama called me every other day, asking if we had our closing date yet.

"Not yet, Mama, but soon," I had to say. There were eight heirs attached to the property who had to sign off on the sale. Seven of them were minors and one of them lived out of state. We had to wait until all of them and their legal guardians were present before we could sign the final escrow papers.

I didn't know during this time that Mama was really ill. In all the times we'd talked, she'd never said a word to me. The day we closed escrow, she was admitted to the hospital. After months of searching and dreaming and praying for our home, she wasn't able to celebrate God's gift to my family. I was very concerned about her health and heartbroken that she had to miss what was meant to be a purely joyful day.

John spent the first night at the new house on his own, making sure everything was set up for us. Friends gathered around us to help us move all our things out of the apartment and into our home. John even made sure our bed was in place and made up.

"I don't want you to have to do anything when you get here," he said. "When you get tired, you can rest without any stress of setting up the bedroom."

His tenderness and care during this time made me fall even more in love with him. I was so happy to finally have my own home, but knowing Mama couldn't be there was weighing on my heart.

My angel had everything moved by early afternoon. The next thing he did was get the grill going. Every day was a good day to barbecue for John. This was the day he became the Beverly Barbecuer. My brother Johnny, the Englewood Barbecuer, joined him. Together, they cooked up ribs and chicken, and of course, Johnny's grilled mutton.

Late that day, some of my siblings made the trip out to the hospital to visit Mama. I was wishing she could have been with us to enjoy in the festive gathering at my home, but her illness robbed us of that opportunity.

Mama was in the hospital for three weeks. Daddy stayed by her bedside, and my siblings and I came to see her often. As the days passed, her condition worsened.

A few days before she passed away, Mama came to me in a dream. She asked me how Daddy was doing. I told her he was fine. After that, I saw a lot of people gathering around her.

Mama loved the Chicago Bulls. I remember they were playing a championship game that Sunday. I was washing my hair, and I said to myself, "I'm washing my hair for my mother's funeral."

The phone rang after a while. It was Daddy saying Mama had gone home to the Lord. He told me that my sisters and I needed to stay home. My brothers were going to accompany him to the hospital to take care of the funeral arrangements.

John and I left our home, picked up Sarah at her house, and then we went to Poopie's house. We girls needed to be together at that time.

We talked and cried for a few hours. Mama's illness and death had been unexpected. We didn't know how to manage life without her daily presence. Trying to process this indescribable feeling was overwhelming. I just was numb all over.

The next day, Daddy asked me to go to the florist with him to pick out flowers and to work with my first cousin Elois to write Mama's obituary. Elois was a rock for us at that time, and if there was one person in our family who knew each family member, it was her.

Daddy shared with me that while the past losses of his mother and other family members had been painful, the pain of losing his wife was a completely different sort of pain. It was an overwhelming loss.

It came to me shortly after that Mama must have known that her time was short. That's why she kept calling and asking about the house. She wanted to see me settled in my own home, and I wanted to see her smile when she saw the house. I'd pictured her sitting on the sun porch, looking over the backyard with us, enjoying this house together. Now I could only imagine it.

Buck and Deacon's

In time, our family settled into a new routine. The kids were traveling by bus and train to schools out of the area, and we continued going to the same church that we had attended while living in the apartment.

I'd actually first gone to that church by accident. A friend of Sarah Ruth's had invited her to visit her church and Sarah had asked me to go with her. John was playing guitar for another church at the time, so it was decided that I would take the kids on my own.

I got to church, but there was no Sarah. So, I called her

after we got home and said, "I missed you at church to-day."

Sarah responded, "I was there, where were you?"

It turned out there were two churches on that corner. I was at one, she was at the other. We had a big laugh about it. She joined me at "the wrong church" the following Sunday, and we both eventually became members there. John followed and was soon playing his guitar for our new home church.

Now, years later, our pastor was visiting our home and asking God to bless it and us.

John was such a proud homeowner. All our ups and downs in the early years of our marriage were paying off big-time. We had room to grow in love and in thanksgiving. We enjoyed hosting big get-togethers, and it seemed that the doorbell never stopped ringing. John got a big grill that he dubbed "Jesse James." It cooked fast. "Jesse James" was the grill of all grills.

The house was in good shape when we bought it, but after a couple of years, it was in need of a new coat of paint. By this time, John was an interior and exterior painting expert, having spent the last few years doing painting jobs on the side. He painted every room in the house and plastered the walls where needed. Even the hardwood floors got a little touchup, so they shone like new.

John started going by one of his nicknames, "Buck." He was a talented perfectionist when it came to his painting and plastering. He expected the same of anyone who worked with him. His brother Raymond worked with him and often commented that his "boss" was too serious for his liking.

John and Daddy, who had completely reconciled by this time, joined forces and started Buck and Deacon's interior and exterior decorating service. At first, Buck painted exteriors of churches, homes, garages, windows. He didn't charge what any of the jobs were worth, but he made sure each was handled expertly and professionally.

Daddy got to the point that he wasn't able to climb ladders to paint, but John couldn't do all the work himself. John was still working full-time for the city. So, he had to schedule his jobs for evenings and weekends. Eventually he had to hire more help to keep up with the clients.

Buck and Deacon's company gave our family more leverage to buy things for the house and take mini vacations. In later years, I told John I wanted to redo our patio, since the backyard was so huge. I drew up a design of how I would like for it to look. He didn't say much at first, but he was very attentive. A few days later, he came to me and told me to pick a landscaping company to lay brick pavers of my liking.

In the meantime, he dug up all the grass where the patio was going to be. I watched him work, thanking God for such a hardworking and caring man, my beloved husband.

Chapter Nine Reflection

Read Psalm 37:34.

Hard work and waiting on God's timing bring the greatest rewards in the end. John and Louise did without and saved for many years so that eventually they were able to purchase their dream home.

Reflect on a time when you did or did not wait for God's best. What was the result? In what areas of your life is God currently leading you to be patient?

Joyful and tragic events are often interwoven in our lives, as Louise experienced. Have you experienced tangible reminders of God's goodness in the midst of a season of grief?

_____

_____

_____

_____

CHAPTER TEN

Music to My Ears

Now therefore write ye this song for you, and teach it the
children of Israel: put it in their mouths, that this song may
be a witness for me against the children of Israel.
—Deuteronomy 31:19

John once said that he was born to sing the blues. He'd picked up his first musical instrument long before I saw him tickling the keys at my childhood church. The great blues legend B.B. King was one of John's inspirations. It was a hard day for him the day Mr. King died.

Buck's family couldn't afford a guitar when he first decided to learn the instrument, so he got his hands on an old, left-handed guitar. He was right-handed, so he taught himself to play the instrument upside down.

Once he could afford a better guitar, Buck only bought top of the line. He always said, "You only live once here, so you should have the best that you can afford."

My husband dedicated hours of his life to learning his musical craft. When he wasn't working and taking care of the family, he had jam sessions at the house with other musicians. Music was a big part of our home, especially on the weekends. Buck played his guitar and I sang.

One weekend before we bought our home, we were sitting in our cozy apartment. The mood was intimate, and John picked up his guitar and began to play. The music was so soothing and personal to me. I couldn't help it; I started to fall to pieces.

The sweet sound of the guitar was like nothing I'd heard before, and the sincerity of the musician behind the music revealed a heart that was like no other. The tears began to drop from my eyes, and I became overwhelmed with emotion and thankfulness for having such a gifted husband and lover—one who didn't just bless me through his acts of service, but who blessed me with his music, too.

Buck didn't just play great blues songs; he wrote them, as well. Some of his songs included his life experiences, the good and the bad. Others were designed to uplift the listener. His songs had a similar form and style, and every single one came from the heart. In addition to playing in the church, he mostly played in local venues around the city, but he traveled to play on occasion, too. Two of his most widely recognized works are "Rock Me Baby" and "Candy Rose."

Buck didn't let his Poor Man's Blues deter him from his melodic dreams. He believed that, with plenty of hard work and prayer, it was just a matter of time before he made a name for himself as one of the most electrifying players in the city.

Buck was not only a musician, but also a gifted music

teacher. He cemented his place in the past, present, and future of the music business through his hard work and through the lives of his students. His decision to focus his talents on gospel music gave him the ability to "blues up" gospel notes, which made him a highly sought-after guitar player.

Life with Buck

Even before I married Buck, I knew he was something else. Buck had aspirations. He never sat still; he was always moving toward a purpose. John had an overwhelming ability to comfort and serve others while walking with authority.

I was fortunate to marry my best friend. We complemented each other in every way. I'm distinctive. He's distinguished.

Buck talked often about the goodness of Jesus and how thankful he was as we grew closer in every aspect of our relationship. As a man in the community, he commanded great respect from everyone he met. He treated those he met with the same respect he wanted from them. This quality of a man is very rare in this day and age.

I consider myself blessed to be able to call myself John's wife. I was his queen, and he was my king.

As I mentioned before, I was a full-time homemaker in the early years of our marriage. That meant I did most of the cooking.

I don't know how Buck and I got to talking about cooking one night, but I think it was after I started working full-time. He told me that once D turned eighteen, we would switch the roles of cooking. I asked if he was serious, and he said, "Hell, yeah." That was the end of the discussion.

Years later, when D was seventeen-and-a-half years old, I said, "Baby, do you remember our conversation years ago, about cooking?"

Buck looked around and slowly said, "Yeah, uh-huh."

"Is seventeen-and-a-half close enough for the swap?"

John said, "Girl, you haven't remembered a lot of our bargains, but you sure remember that." We both almost fell out laughing.

Buck held up his end of the bargain. After that night, he did all the cooking and his dishes surpassed my own. I told him more than once he was doing too much for me all the time.

He told me, "No, you are my wife, my queen." He also said, "God will hold me accountable if I don't take care of you and my family."

I said before that Buck was called the Beverly Barbecuer. There was a reason for it. He showed off his skills all year long, from his ribs to his amazing sauces. He even made a breakfast that would put any restaurant to shame.

If you wanted a fried turkey for the holidays, Buck was the man to talk to. Orders for his fried turkey came in early from friends and family for the holidays and special occasions. Our home was filled with turkeys, gallons and gallons of cooking oil, and many aluminum pans, not to mention injectors and seasonings. The aroma filled the house until we started to smell like turkey, too.

There was so much traffic in and out of that front door during these times. It was a joy to see how Buck put smiles on his customers' faces. I could only envision the conversations around their dinner tables while they ate a slice of Buck's turkey.

The Art of Cooking

Cooking is like painting or writing a song. Just as there are so many notes and colors, there are only so many flavors. It's how Buck combined them that set him apart.

The combination of flavors made his gumbo unique. Somehow, the neighbors always knew when he was cooking that dish. They said the smell came through the bricks from our house into theirs. After a while, they were at the front door, asking, "You haven't forgotten about us, have you?"

Buck replied, "No, not at all. I got something else for you, as well. Just go back home and give me a minute, I will bring the food over."

Sure enough, he packed up a few dishes of what he had prepared and went out, cheerfully giving.

At one point, Buck decided he wanted to give baking a serious go. So, one day, while we were out shopping, he wandered off into the appliance section of the store. He looked at about all the mixers, some larger and others small, ranging in prices.

Knowing my husband, whatever mixer he landed on, it would need to perform top-notch, because it was going to have to work for all types. He eventually found what he was looking for online: a dark red Kitchen-Aid.

Buck was in the man cave upstairs the day his new toy arrived. The carrier was kind enough to carry the heavy box inside for me. I closed the door and called for Buck to come down from the cave.

You could see the excitement all over his face as he placed the box on the dining room table and began to unravel layers of cardboard, foam, and plastic. He admired his Kitchen-Aid for a while; then, he looked for a spot in the kitchen to place it. Within a day or two, he began baking after work,

He baked key lime pies, pound cakes, peanut butter cookies, butter cookies, and peach cobbler, among other desserts and treats. He came home from work and baked at least twice a week.

As with everything else Buck did, he wanted perfection in his baking skills. His cookies were excellent. I immediately went back to memories of grade school whenever the aroma of his cookies filled the house. I couldn't wait for them to come out of the oven. Neither could our grandsons.

Chapter Ten Reflection

Read 1 Corinthians 10:31.

God has given each person talents and gifts that should be used to serve others and glorify Him.

Buck used his musical abilities, as well as his culinary talents, to minister to others.

With what interests, talents, or abilities has God gifted you, and how are you using them to encourage the church, reach the lost, and glorify God?

_____

_____

_____

_____

_____

_____

CHAPTER ELEVEN

You Are Somebody

Be ye strong therefore, and let not your hands be weak: for your work shall be rewarded.
—*2 Chronicles 15:7*

We each have our own way of showing our love for others. My angel showed his love through acts of service and gift-giving. John was always finding little ways to let me know how much he cared for me. Big box, little box, sweet, or treat—I usually found them on my bed, right on my pillow. Mr. Somebody was always listening, even when I didn't think he was. The little pop-up surprises continually reminded me of that.

Buck usually picked me up after work, unless he had another side job going on. One Saturday, I got into our Jeep and noticed the aroma of food. But I didn't see any, so I kept looking back, trying to find what I was smelling. After a while, I asked, "Baby, is there food in here?"

Buck shrugged it off and said he'd had a bite to eat earlier. I probably was smelling the lingering odor. A little farther down the road, he said, "I got to stop and drop something off at my friend's. I know you are tired, but it won't take long."

He didn't mention the friend's name, and I wasn't familiar with the area we were in, so I started thinking through all the people we knew who might live out this way. No one was coming to mind.

We were traveling east—and far east at that. John was dressed in light, relaxing clothing and it was a warm summer day, so I was in a comfortable, casual work attire.

He told me we were almost there, but I didn't see any houses. It was all park recreation land, along with driving paths. I looked around and around, unable to see our destination, but Buck looked like he knew exactly where he was going. This was another one of his special gifts to me.

I had purchased a picnic basket that reminded me of the one my mother had when I was growing up. It had been sitting on the top shelf of our pantry, and I had looked up at it from time to time, hoping one day it would be used for a romantic scene with the two of us. I began to realize that that day had finally arrived.

My eyes filled with tears as I once again fell in love with the man sitting next to me. Buck opened the back of the Jeep, where he had the blanket covering the picnic basket and the small cooler. He spread out the blanket and set the basket and cooler nearby.

After walking back to the Jeep, John opened the door and reached for my hand, leading me to the blanket on the hill overlooking the water. The basket contained sandwiches from our favorite sandwich shop, cheese and crackers, and grapes and strawberries. The cooler contained fine wine, soda, and water.

I sat there feeling shock and joy at the blessing this day was ending on. We rested on the blanket for some time, enjoying one another. Later, we walked along the water holding hands and smiling.

I never wanted that night to end. I wanted to stay there, just the two of us in that calm, restful place. *Life is good*, I thought over and over. We made a promise to go back to that park in the summers to come.

Buck was always reminding me that he is somebody. And so am I. His love points me to my Savior, who made the ultimate sacrifice to show His unconditional love for me. Buck lives out God's calling for us to love one another so well. Buck's example makes me, and others, see Christ more clearly.

Chapter Eleven Reflection

Read 1 John 4:12.

How you love another person helps them understand God's love for them.

John delighted in expressing his love for Louise with tangible gifts and investments of his time and talents.

How can you demonstrate your love for your spouse (or another family member) this week? Plan a surprise that will be meaningful to your loved one and which will reflect to them the love God has for them.

_____

_____

_____

_____

_____

_____

CHAPTER TWELVE

He Never Promised Me a Rose Garden

*And the L*ORD *God planted a garden eastward in Eden; and there he put the man whom he had formed.*
—Genesis 2:8

What is nature? Is it plants, animals, the landscape? It's all these things and more. God is the Creator of it all, which means He's the best of the best. He creates the template, and we, as His children, imitate His masterpiece.

Let's apply this metaphor to our backyard, a space filled with high weeds, dead brown grass, overgrown trees, broken-down fencing, and a rusting swing set in the middle of that mess. What an uninviting eyesore.

This was the canvas Buck and I had to work with when we became homeowners. Our large yard was a beast of a project that could have been overwhelming, but we set to work, chopping down weeds and dead trees.

Then came the rainy season, and the weeds sprang right back up. It felt like all our work had been for nothing. One day, we visited a family friend, Ella Mae Moss, who was a gardener. She had a fairly large backyard filled with beautiful plants and flowers. You could tell by looking at them that she particularly loved red and white flowers. Scattered throughout the yard were life-sized ceramic animals.

While visiting Ella Mae, we started talking about gardening and how nature required lots of cultivating, just like our lives did. Buck and I wanted to turn our calamity of a yard into an oasis; we just didn't know the best way to start. Mama Moss gave us our first lesson in gardening that day. The words she spoke to us changed how we looked at our mountain of a project.

Like Ella Mae, Buck loved red and white flowers. We were determined to transform our yard into a beautiful place. As we grew in our home, so did our garden. Instead of being an eyesore, it became an inviting space—and not just to humans. It drew in birds and lots of butterflies during the spring and summer.

Buck also shared my Mama's love of roses. On some of our days off, we visited the plant nurseries around the city. Sometimes Buck made a stop on his way home from work and picked up another rosebush for our garden. It took time and patience, but, eventually, we began seeing the fruit of our labor.

There's something healing about working in the dirt and breathing in the fresh air while the warmth of the sun falls on your shoulders. God has a way of giving us peace and tranquility as we work the soil of the land.

Buck created a walk-through garden, as long as the house and as wide as a driveway, that was visible from the street. Passersby commented on the beauty of the garden where John had all the perennials planted. Like Mama, he added a rosebush or two to his garden each year, until he had a flowering rainbow.

My garden was in the backyard, at the base of a maple tree. In the late spring, we cleaned up the maple seeds that had fallen from the tree and Buck tilled up the soil for my annuals. We worked knee-by-knee, Buck digging the hole for me to place each of my colorful new impatiens. I loved the beautiful colors the flowers created in the yard—the reds, the whites, the lilac, the orange. And that was just the beginning.

There was a lot of buzz about our garden throughout the year. The neighbors waited with anticipation each season to capture the essence of our garden, bringing their children and grandchildren by to see it. Some neighbors called one area of our gardens the Japanese garden.

Our partnership gardening eventually caught on with the neighbors. When one of our neighbors got married, he and his wife started planting their own oasis together. You could say Buck and I were considered the trailblazers on the block.

Relaxing in nature is a beautiful sight. Watching the living things grow and discovering the creatures each plant attracts fills the heart with wonder and awe.

At one point in our lives, John and I only shared one day off together. During those spring and summer months, he occasionally picked flowers from the garden and placed them in a vase on my bedside table while I was at work, just to let me know he loved me and was thinking of me.

One early summer day, we had a few vacation days together. We were working in the yard when one of our neighbors approached us from side yard by the front of the house.

I saw he had three people with him, admiring the garden. He asked if it was okay for them to come around to enter the backyard. We both replied, yes, of course. Once they joined us, he introduced us to the people. It turned out they had lived in the house before us, years ago. The young lady in the group stated she remembered her grandmother gardening in that very spot, and she began to cry.

She was overjoyed to find the garden being restored in such a way. We gave her a hug and invited all of them to come back and meet the entire family at an upcoming Sunday family dinner. They were very thankful for the invitation, but they had traveled from California and would be returning home before Sunday. They thanked us again before leaving for letting them visit a childhood memory and for caring so well for their grandmother's former home.

Buck and I spent most of our free time in the yard when the weather permitted. He would often sit across from me, with my feet in his lap as he massaged them, catching up on things and planning for the future in the garden that he had never promised, but still gave me. The rose garden that God had given to us.

Chapter Twelve Reflection

Read Genesis 2:15.

Humanity's first assigned task was to take care of God's creation, specifically the garden of Eden.

John and Louise worked hard to care for the piece of this earth that God entrusted to them and to make it an oasis for their family and others.

How are you engaged in caring for God's creation—that which you may own as well as general stewardship of the earth?

_____

_____

_____

_____

_____

_____

CHAPTER THIRTEEN

Family Dinners and Birthday Surprises

The table is a place to remember the blessings of God. Family dinners are a time to gather with family and friends for the purpose of enjoying a meal as both a gift and a means of grace.

Buck's brother first had the idea to host a monthly family dinner after his son accepted Christ as his Savior and was baptized.

It was a very heartfelt dinner, and at that time in our lives, this gathering was needed. It brought us together for two common goals, which were love and family. Both were always there, but as with the garden, they needed constant care and cultivation.

After this first Sunday dinner, we decided each family would take turns hosting a family meal on the first Sunday of each month. In the beginning, there were six households in the family who took turns hosting. From time to time we had family dinners out, at the discretion of the host of the month. We also have had some potluck dinners over the years.

You never knew what was going to be on the menu to eat, and that was exciting in and of itself. However, there was also the anticipation of being all together as one family. It was a time to get caught up on family news, to play games, to laugh and cry, and to pray and be thankful for God's grace and mercy. Family dinner gave us a chance to celebrate achievements and milestones, and to support each other in our various activities or endeavors.

Because there were enough of us, each family hosted the family dinner about twice a year. Buck and I started planning out the menu at least two weeks in advance when our turn came around. Once we'd finalize the menu, Buck went and added about five more things to the menu before the dinner.

After a while, I started saying, "Why don't you just plan out the dinner yourself, sweetie? You're just going to change it anyway."

It never failed; he replied, "No, baby, I need your help." Always a sucker for him, I put my two cents in, knowing that Boo was going to make the final menu on his own.

Buck enjoyed hosting for the family, from the adults to the youngest. He wanted everyone to remember family, beginning with prayer, followed by good food, drink, and great conversations.

The men of the family showcased their cooking skills at some of the dinners. The food ranged from barbecue, skirts steaks, pot roast, pasta, oxtail soup, and string beans, to chicken dishes. The women of the family were sitting back, chilling as we watched them complete their dishes with confidence and pride.

One highlight of the dinners that we will always, and I mean *always*, remember is a married couple who always gave us a show when they were around. They're affectionately known as Cookie and Bozo when performing.

I've had the privilege of knowing them for many years now, and they have become more comical as time goes by.

They said that, as young married couple, they made fun of the husband's uncle and auntie, who fussed and cussed all the time. They now laugh a lot about those days because they've become that couple.

Bozo jokes that he can't even say good morning properly these days, and Cookie says she doesn't hold back what she's thinking anymore. That's just life.

In connection with these family dinners, we also created a monthly newsletter we send to all our family members. It helps us stay up-to-date on graduations, births, weddings, performing arts, sports, family reunions, and other accomplishments. It is especially helpful for family who live out of state.

We've had many other families and friends break bread with us at these family dinners over the years. Some of them are surprised that we've managed to keep the dinners going as long as we have. We hold these dinners dear to our hearts, while we yet live, and we thank Jesus for this precious family of ours.

Reflecting on these family dinners that have been going on for so many years, I am in awe of God's faithfulness to me. I have been blessed by the mighty hands of God all my life. I live to thank God for letting me see another year after year, with His grace and mercy.

I make it a point not to work on the week around my birthday. I see it as a time of celebration and thanksgiving. We tend to make a big deal about certain birthdays, like twenty-one and thirty, but the ones in between often go overlooked. For me, however, every birthday is special and worthy of celebration.

Every year, I start asking myself how I'm going to celebrate as my birthday approaches. I've had some small parties through the years, but there are two things I know for certain—one is that I am not going to work on that day, and the other is that I'm going to look cute.

Before my forty-eighth birthday, Keshia casually asked about one of my coworkers whom I spoke about often. I didn't think much of it at first, but then I started to wonder if they were starting to plan something for me at work. I hoped not, because as anybody who knows me is aware of, working on my birthday was out of the question.

As the day approached, one of my sisters asked what I was going to do. I had no clue. No one was telling me they'd made plans for a celebration, and I was starting to feel downright lonely.

The day of my birthday dawned with me planning to sleep in. Buck suggested I break with tradition, make myself look pretty, but go on into the office. That was not what I wanted to hear.

Can you believe he somehow talked me into going to work anyway? He promised to pick me up on time and take me to dinner after work, so now I was thinking that there was a surprise waiting for me after all.

My daughter called me up and asked what I'd planned on wearing to dinner. I replied, "Well, something black, I guess." I asked her, "Why, what's the big deal?"

She passed it off by saying that Buck was coming home for lunch and she wanted to make sure he had my clothes with him when he came to pick me up.

When I arrived at work, the officer at the door said, "Good morning." I gave him a look and said back, "It's my birthday. I shouldn't be here," and I kept on walking.

As the day went on, my phone kept ringing with questions from my family. "What are you doing?" they asked. "When are you leaving?" They even asked what I was going to wear.

As promised, Buck was right on time. He drove us downtown, to a hotel with valet parking. I kept asking question after question, but he wouldn't say a thing.

We checked in, got to our suite, and he suggested I just relax while he ran downstairs to grab us a sandwich to tide us over until dinner. I still had no idea what in the world he was up to.

Inside the room, rose petals were everywhere. It looked like something out of a fairy tale. I was giggling when Buck got back with the sandwiches, which ended up tasting awful!

He kept sneaking looks at his watch while I was getting ready for dinner, but I saw him every time. Something was up. I just didn't know what.

We left the hotel once we were both ready, and he drove us over near Soldier Field, then left me waiting in the car for about five minutes. When he got back to the car, he drove us over to Burnham Harbor at Lake Shore

Drive, Chicago. He walked me over to a gated area on the dock and surprised me when he entered the combination on the lock.

The harbor was quiet. The sun was setting, and a yacht was tied up at the end of the dock.

"Baby, are we going out on the water?" I asked.

He said, "Yeah you are."

Once we got closer, my family and friends started screaming and singing "Happy Birthday." Forty-eight roses were waiting for me on the deck. I had my best friend beside me and the people I loved the most all around me. I felt like a celebrity with all the bells and whistles. I spent most of the night on the deck as we sailed over Lake Michigan, watching the water flow under my feet.

When I think about that night, I'm reminded yet again that I am truly blessed beyond measure.

Chapter Thirteen Reflection

Read 1 Peter 4:9.

The art of hospitality is a way to show God's love, build strong relationships, and create lasting memories.

The Buckners used their home and their gift of hospitality to host regular family gatherings and celebrations.

How and when can you exercise hospitality? Whom is God leading you to invite into your home and life, and how can your welcome show them God's own acceptance?

_____

_____

_____

_____

_____

_____

CHAPTER FOURTEEN

Our Church Home

I call heaven and earth to record this day against you, that I have set before you life and death, blessing and cursing: therefore choose life, that both thou and thy seed may live...

—Deuteronomy 30:19

Choosing a church is a very important decision that will affect one's entire family deeply. It had been ten years since my angel visited Mount Hermon Missionary Baptist on the South Side of Chicago. I'd had to work that day, so he came to pick me up after the service.

He always made it a point to look his absolute best on Sundays. Part of it was just him; part of it was because he played guitar for different churches and he said that a performer always had to look good.

On the Sundays I worked, I left before he got dressed for church. On occasion, my coworkers would rush to the office work floor after seeing him on Sundays, saying, "Louise, your husband is looking good," over and over again. This particular Sunday was no different.

I wanted to know how his visit went, but I got distracted by my coworkers. *What is he wearing now?* I wondered as I signed off my computer, grabbed my personal things, and headed for the door.

Buck was pleased with how the worship service had gone. Anytime my angel would praise the Lord with his guitar, he came out of the service uplifted. He talked about how the choirs sung and the preacher preached. He said he felt the Spirit in the place, and that he looked forward to visiting again soon.

A few weeks later, Buck told me he was thinking about playing for Mount Hermon on a regular basis, which he had done in many churches before. Not long after, he was given the right hand of fellowship and became a member of their church.

I was a member at another church, when my work schedule permitted me to attend. Buck had been a member of that other church, as well. I was hesitant to join Mount Hermon, because I knew musicians never stayed in the same place for long. Buck was no exception. So, instead of joining the church, I just visited Mount Hermon on occasion. It was a traditional Baptist church, similar to the one in which I'd grown up.

As time went on, I often asked how church had been after he got home. His report was always that it was great. He felt like he'd become part of the church family and that the congregation had embraced him as Christians ought to do.

He felt like he could be himself there, and he felt true joy serving through his musical giftings there. Men's Day was one of his favorite events of the year. Buck wanted the men to shine, to sing with confidence and power.

A Church to Call Home

Buck and his guitar were part of a number of musicals performed at the churches in the Chicago area. Mount Hermon was no different. He listened to the music tracks from the music directors and spend hours preparing for the big event each time.

I remember once Pastor Moses from Mount Hermon was going to be teaching down in Louisiana. Deacon Walton was going to drive down, and he asked Buck if he'd be a second driver. I love getaways and we have family down in Baton Rouge, so Buck suggested this would be a good time to visit.

I got to know a number of people from Boo's church during that trip, and not long after we got back to Chicago, members from Mount Hermon started approaching me, asking me when I was going to join them.

It was a beautiful day in June when I got myself up from the pew and joined Mount Hermon. It was one of those rare Sundays when I didn't have to work, and Buck had convinced me to go to church with him. After years of searching, he'd finally found a church he could call home, and I was thrilled that we could share that experience together again.

Boo and others always told me that I have so much to offer God's people. When my schedule permitted, I attended church on Sundays.

Mount Hermon has a man of God at the helm in Pastor

Moses, and the church has many ministries led by Bible-believing members. It's an amazing feeling when you love your church family and they love you back. There's joy to be found in walking together on the same road to glory. Sanctification is an amazing journey that isn't meant to be walked alone. I am so grateful that Mount Hermon provided a place for us to walk this road with others.

WORKBOOK

Chapter Fourteen Reflection

Read Hebrews 10:25.

Being connected to a church provides a place to worship, grow, and serve.

The Buckners found great joy and fulfillment in being a part of their church.

Are you connected with a local congregation and are you faithful in attendance? If not, how can you begin the process of finding a fellowship to join?

_____

_____

_____

_____

_____

_____

_____

CHAPTER FIFTEEN

Love Is Where the Heart Is

Serve the LORD with gladness: come before his presence with singing. Know yea that the LORD he is God. It is that hath made us, and not we ourselves; we are his people, and the sheep of his pasture.

For the LORD is good; his mercy is everlasting; and his truth endureth to all generations.
—Psalm 100:2–3, 5

Christmas was a magical season for my angel. Out of all the days in the year, it brought the biggest dazzle to his beautiful eyes. Boo looked forward to everything about Christmas, including the gathering of family, the shopping for presents, the food, and the opening of the gifts. I remember many times we went shopping at the tree lots for a live Christmas tree.

Boo wanted our little family to pick out the perfect tree. We walked the lot and looked up the trees and down the trees, searching for the perfect width, height, and fullness. If we didn't find the perfect tree at one lot, we went to the next.

Buck had a unique collection of ornaments we'd gathered over the years. Some ornaments were found at thrift shops, some were from Marshfield's or antique shops. John was always keeping his eye out for ornaments. His collection didn't end with just tree ornaments; he had ceramic houses and buildings, including a church and a library that we set up as a winter village each year.

I strung popcorn to make garlands to adorn the tree. This process was relaxing, inexpensive, and beautiful. Once we put the popcorn garland on the tree, we strung the lights and hung the assortment of ornaments. Once we were done, we stepped back to smell the live tree and admire its beauty.

Buck had a habit of rearranging things after the rest of us went to bed. I don't think he ever knew we knew he was doing it. I used to think it was just something he did, but I've discovered it's pretty common in other families, as well. Isn't that funny?

John loved watching the kids run to the tree early Christmas mornings. Those moments made his heart sing. Taking them to see Santa when they were small was a delight for him as well as for the kids. I saw it as another chance for him and the kids to have some bonding time.

Being a gift-giver by nature, Buck always went out of his way to make Christmas extra-special for the kids. I remember one year when he got our son a fire truck that he really wanted. An expletive slipped out when he saw the fire truck. We had the hardest time not laughing when we heard the word. We didn't want to encourage him to say it again.

Any parent knows what a test of patience assembling Christmas gifts can be. Buck and I often worked late into the night, trying to get everything ready in time. Some of these projects were more than we bargained for, between our work schedules and waiting for the kids to go to bed. I read through the instructions and Buck worked the tools. Somehow, we always made it, and the end result was always worth it.

Buck and I loved entertaining guests in our home. One year, after the kids were grown, he decided we should have a big Christmas extravaganza. I jumped onto the idea right away.

Then I remembered all the times our kids had begged us not to throw any more parties because they were tired of helping with all the preparations. This time we started planning in advance, so the kids would have nothing to do but to show up with their children.

I knew the party had been on Buck's mind for a while because he had it well planned before we even started working out the details—from the food to shopping for gifts for all invited. That's another reason we had the bond we shared; we both loved making people happy in our home.

We set the day of the party for Christmas Eve, starting at noon and ending at four. The tree was looking its best. The house was festive all over with fruit baskets and holiday singing, and people covered the house from front to back and up and down.

As each guest departed, they got to choose a gift from under the tree. I couldn't help but thank God for blessing us with another gathering of family and friends.

WORKBOOK

Chapter Fifteen Reflection

Read Philippians 4:4.

While holidays can be a lot of work, the more that you invest of yourself in giving, the greater joy you receive.

John and Louise worked hard to make Christmas a memorable and joyful time for their family and friends.

Do you see holidays as a time of joy and giving, or as something else you "have to do"? How can you avoid turning seasons of celebration into a burden?

_____

_____

_____

_____

_____

_____

_____

CHAPTER SIXTEEN

The Salvation Army

*And let us not be weary in well doing: for in due season we
shall reap, if we faint not.*
                                                    —Galatians 6:9

I feel it's important to give back to the community in
which I live. I have always wanted to serve my fellowman,
but for the longest time, I wasn't sure how I could do so.

In the early 2000s, God blessed our community with
the Salvation Army Ray and Joan Kroc Corps Community
Center, a multimillion-dollar, state-of-the-art facility built
by the Salvation Army to serve people of all backgrounds,
with a focus on underserved populations.

This massive structure was built thanks to a fund cre-
ated by the late Joan Kroc, wife of McDonald's franchiser
Ray Kroc. Due to her generosity, there are several of these
Salvation Army-run centers in cities throughout the
United States.

Once I heard about the center and the chance to volunteer for duty, I knew this was the opportunity for which

I'd been waiting.

I contacted the volunteer liaison at the center, who helped me fill out the volunteer form online. After the center performed a background check and I got clearance, we scheduled a meeting.

The volunteer coordinator greeted me with a warm smile and a handshake. She seemed very pleasant, and not long into the conversation, I found her to be a God-fearing, Bible-believing individual. She told me about an orientation for new volunteer candidates that I'd have to take before being able to volunteer at any Salvation Army facility.

I went through the four-hour class about two weeks later and was issued my certificate of completion. Then I began participating in a variety of volunteer opportunities. John likes to tease me when we pass the Kroc Center, calling it my second home. One time, he joked, "Baby, you done went and joined the foreign legion." I always respond to his jests with a laugh. I've learned that volunteering is a good way to learn new skills and better myself. It's also very rewarding. It leaves me with a feeling of being a small part of a larger whole, working to make my city a better home for the people living in it. Serving others is something we all should be doing. It's something that we're called to do as followers of Christ.

If you have a chance to volunteer at a church, community center, school, park district, library, or human service agency, I recommend doing so. Your voice and your presence are very much needed.

Chapter Sixteen Reflection

Read Galatians 6:9.

Each person should use their time and talents to "give back" to the community.

Louise found purpose and satisfaction by serving as a volunteer to help those in need.

In what ways are you involved in serving your community, particularly the poor and marginalized? If you have never helped in this way, what is one way you could volunteer? Plan one event that you can assist at to get an idea if it is a program you could participate in regularly.

_____

_____

_____

_____

_____

CHAPTER SEVENTEEN

Homecomings

This is a faithful saying, and worthy of all acceptation, that Christ Jesus came into the world to save sinners; of whom I am chief.

Howbeit for this cause I obtained mercy, that in me first Jesus Christ might shew forth all longsuffering, for a pattern to them which should hereafter believe on him to life everlasting.

Now unto the King eternal, immortal, invisible, the only wise God, be honour and glory for ever and ever. Amen.
—1 Timothy 1:15–17

When Daddy's kidneys started failing, he started going to dialysis three times a week. He took up with a woman he met at the dialysis center, who was also a patient. I first found out about her through some other family members.

She was not like my mother at all. At first, I was surprised that Daddy had chosen another woman. I was even more surprised that she was so different from Mama. Daddy said she was six months younger than me, and he bragged about that. Looking at her, though, you would have thought she was six years older.

She came over a time or two and sat right up under Daddy. We didn't talk much, she and I, but she didn't seem to have any trouble talking to Buck.

I treated her with respect, but for some reason, Daddy decided he was going to have his fun at my expense. I bit my tongue for as long as I could, but I was so upset about being disrespected by my father in my home that I left the gathering and retired to my bedroom to cry. I never came back out while they were there.

Despite the hurt Daddy caused, I still visited him in my childhood home, where he was living with my brother Riley, who served as his caregiver. Daddy's illness resulted in several surgeries, and I visited him in the hospital throughout his stays. Buck and I assisted in any way we could.

Riley was admitted to the hospital on a few occasions during this time, as well. At the time, we thought it was due to exhaustion from caring for Daddy. We found out later that it was something more.

> *For we know that if our earthly house of this tabernacle were dissolved, we have a building of God, a house not made with hands, eternal in the heavens.*
> **—2 Corinthians 5:1**

Daddy was called home in May 2008. We laid him to rest next to our mama. His passing caused some hardship between my siblings. There were some objections to how Daddy had spelled out his will. This upheaval lasted a few years and ended up in court hearings. There were no true winners, and the bitter taste of strife will hang around awhile before sweetness takes over again. Some of Daddy's buildings ended up on the auction block, being sold for next to nothing. None of us live on the former family properties, and two of the buildings are sitting vacant and deteriorating.

The Doorkeeper

About five years after Daddy died, my brother Riley started to make a lot of doctors' visits. He was losing weight and his doctor said it was his thyroid, so the doctor treated him for that. After a year, there was no improvement, so the doctor brought in a specialist.

It was decided that Riley would be transferred to a leading and innovative hospital in the medical district in Chicago. After a few days and more tests, the medical team determined Riley had a rare disease. Those of us who were close enough were called to the hospital to meet with the doctor. The news he gave us wasn't good.

When we got to Riley's room, he told us he already knew what was going on. He'd once visited someone from his church on that very hospital floor with the same condition.

Riley stayed in the hospital for two months. I eventually got a call from the hospital, letting me know he was going on life support, but that he was still conscious. I rushed to the hospital to speak to my brother, along with my siblings and other family members. I bent down and spoke into Riley's ear to be sure of what he wanted. I asked the question several times to make sure we both were communicating clearly. Each time he nodded to say yes. He was on life support for a day or two before the tube was finally removed.

I went to see Riley after work on the day the tube was removed. My son, Darnell, was already there. He met me outside the room and told me that Uncle Riley was hoarse from the tube, but he was talking up a storm.

Riley's pastor visited often. Each time, Riley would say, "Give it to me," just as his pastor entered the room. He meant, "Give me the Word of God."

I noticed a missed call from the hospital the day Riley joined our parents. I called back at once and was told he'd made the transition already. I called my older brother, Solo, to let him know. It so happened that Solo and his wife were at their house of worship nearby. Solo told me to stay home, that he would take care of things at the hospital.

Riley is laid to rest near the gate of the same cemetery in which Mama and Daddy were laid to rest. Some of Mama's family is there, too. I like to say that Riley is still ushering others in at the gate, just as he did in his church for so long. Even in death, he is still the doorkeeper.

WORKBOOK

Chapter Seventeen Reflection

Read 1 Thessalonians 4:13.

The sure promise of heaven gives believers hope even in death.

Louise sorrowed at the deaths of her father and brother but knew that because of their faith in Christ, she would be reunited with them in heaven.

How is grief different for believers than for unbelievers? Does the knowledge that each person will face death motivate you to share Christ with those who do not know Him?

_____

_____

_____

_____

_____

CHAPTER EIGHTEEN

Our Growing Family Tree

Only take heed to thyself, and keep thy soul diligently, lest thou forget the things which thine eyes have seen, and lest they depart from thy heart all the days of thy life: but teach them thy sons and thy sons' sons...
—Deuteronomy 4:9

Buck and I have been blessed with five grandkids. Four are related by blood, and one is related by love. All of them are precious parts of our lives.

The Joy of My Heart

Jalen Jay Smith, better known as Jay, or JJ, is our firstborn grandchild. He spent his infant and toddler years with us, and I was so happy to have our first grandchild living under our roof. He brought new life into the household.

LaKeshia was attending college when she became pregnant. I noticed she became more withdrawn and her personality changed. My mother's instinct was in full swing.

I sat down next to her on her bed one day and said, "Baby, we need to talk."

Not long after we started talking, I asked her if she was pregnant, and she answered that she was. I knew some of what she was feeling, and I told her she needed to get up and out of the house because being isolated would do her no good. We went for a walk together, and I told her about my two pregnancies and how she and her brother had been born. Along the walk, I discussed healthy eating and pre-natal care with her. I watched her countenance change during the walk. Soon, she was behaving more like the young woman I knew that she was.

Keshia continued with her education after JJ's birth. Some in the family doubted she had what it took to be a mother and still attend school. She quickly proved them wrong.

Jalen is the joy of my heart, but he and Buck were inseparable. He was about three years old when he started his first building project with his granddaddy—a desk with shelving for my computer.

There was one time when Buck took JJ with him to the police station to pick up his paycheck. Jalen watched the officers walking around the station with guns on their sides for a while. Then he looked up and said, "Grand-daddy, let's get the hell out of here."

He was about four at the time. I remember laughing my butt off when Buck told me the story.

Keshia and Jalen's father got married when Jalen wasn't much more than four years old. The first thing he asked for was for a little brother. It didn't take long for his wish to be fulfilled. I was thrilled when Keshia shared the news with me, especially because it meant JJ wouldn't grow up alone.

JJ has been the lead soloist in church, singing in the youth and junior choirs. His mother has spent time and money making sure he and his brother are well rounded in both education and culture.

Jay is very interested in music and drama. He started acting on stage when he was seven, and he was chosen to sing the national anthem at his graduation. Buck called him little Sidney Poitier, but his chosen stage name is Jay Diamond. Like his granddaddy, Jay likes to write songs and he's taken up choreography. He's is a highly ambitious young man, determined to make the world a better place.

My Sports Fanatic

Jamil Ahman Smith, better known as Millie or Jam, is my sports fanatic. Ever since he was a baby, he's had a football or a basketball in his hands. As he grew up, he added roller skates, skateboards, and hockey sticks—you get the picture. Where there is action or fast-moving things, you'll find Jam.

Jamil liked sweets and naps when he was little. It seemed like, one way or another, he was always napping. He's a very finicky eater. He's got to touch, smell, and give food a good look-over before he'll attempt to taste it. Good cornbread and crackers are the exceptions: leave him alone and he'll eat the whole pan or entire sleeves, respectively, of those two items. His mama's baked beans are right up there, too.

Jam's an avid basketball player. Buck spent hours in the summer watching him practice. All that hard work paid off, when out of eighty-plus young people who tried out for the team his first year, he made the top ten. Like many kids his age, he is also a video game enthusiast.

> *Train up a child in the way he should go: and when he is old, he will not depart from it.*
> **—Proverbs 22:6**

My Bonus Grandson

Elijah Jaden Ivy, nicknamed EJ, is my bonus grandson. He entered our lives at a young age. Our son, Darnell, and his mother attended college together and began seeing each other after EJ's mother and father called things off. EJ is very smart when it comes to academics, and he's made honor roll each year of school. He's also very tall, reaching six feet before entering high school.

He has played on the football and basketball teams at his school. He and Jamil enjoy challenging each other in basketball and video games.

My Only Granddaughter

Chloe Danielle Buckner, whom I call Clo-Clo Chanel, is my one and only granddaughter—my darling, beautiful, talkative, bossy granddaughter. I told her parents she was going to be a big talker the first time I saw her after she was born. In her young life, she's had several modeling engagements, has taken ballet, and has served as the poster child for My Life Matters.

She looks like a doll of color with lots of long, wavy hair. I had that same look when I was a child. She is bursting with personality, questions, individuality, and independence. She loves fashion and being a girly-girl. Her great-grandmother was just the same, so she gets that honestly. She's fond of the word *actually*.

Whenever Chloe and I get together, it's nail spa time. She loves the color purple for her nails, and I enjoy spa time with her. It reminds me of all the times growing up when Mama, my sisters, and I did our nails together. Those were times of female bonding, and I am honored to experience the same with my granddaughter. It means the world to me to share this experience with Chloe, and she adores this time with me, as well. She's just a little impatient for her nails to dry.

Chloe dubbed Buck "Papa John." Slurpees were their special treat together. I'm pretty sure Buck introduced them to her first. Strawberry and cherry were his two favorites. Now they're hers.

Chloe is a family person. She knows everybody, and everybody knows her. She's a caring girl who wants the best for everyone. She loves to snuggle up with me on her visits. Unlike her cousin and younger brother, she's never had an issue with eating. I don't cook much for myself, but I make an exception for these kids. Buck would say, "The grandchildren must be coming over—you're cooking."

Now that she's older, Clo-Clo is modeling for several agencies. She wants to be a model and a singer.

My Youngest Grandson

Camron Westly Buckner is better known as Cam. Cam is easy on the eyes, and he's been on the go since he arrived. Gymnastics fits him perfectly since he loves to climb, jump, and run. He is so independent-minded! He's said that he never wants to be a baby; he wants to be his own person.

Cam went the first five years of his life without a haircut. His hair was so long and soft, so strangers often mistook him for a girl. Cam, being very vocal, said in his young, raspy voice, "Hey, could you look at what I am wearing before speaking?"

His energy level is either at zero or ten. When it's zero, he's sleeping. The second he wakes, he's good to go. Always active, he's involved in wrestling, and he loves sports figures and cars.

My youngest grandson is very picky about his eating habits. Bread is not ever on his radar.

Like Clo-Clo, he's started his model career. When you're as handsome as he is, why not? He also enjoys spending time with his father. Cam calls it "man time."

It's impossible to slow down with so much vitality all around me. My grandchildren are the youth of my heart and mind.

Chapter Eighteen Reflection

Read Proverbs 17:6.

Grandchildren are a sweet reward of old age!

Louise and John were blessed with several grandchildren and worked hard to be an example of character and faith for them.

If you have grandchildren, how are you investing in their lives, not just with gifts or fun times, but also with being an example for them in the faith?

_____

_____

_____

_____

_____

_____

CHAPTER NINETEEN

A Celebration of Life— Yes, for You, My Angel

How do you celebrate an angel? A person who gives so much of himself to others, without looking for any earthly rewards? It should be a joyful and spirit-filled celebration. It should include the things that bring him happiness. Boo loves the Lord, lots of uplifting music, and singing. So, I decided to give him a gospel musical celebration of life for his birthday...

This was going to be a well-thought-out plan for me, and it would require many players. So, I set out to make it a very spiritual celebration of life for my angel. I contacted the Salvation Army in Blue Island, Illinois, to see if the sanctuary would be available on October 8. My Angel was almost superstitious about doing things on his birthdate, October 7, because he said people always passed away near their birthdate. He always wanted to be settled somewhere quietly.

The Salvation Army was booked on the eighth of the

month, but the day before—October 7—was open. My good friend Barbara and I took a chance and booked the date, praying that I would be able to get Boo out of the house for that evening. After that, I had to get a program together and hire a caterer.

I recruited Buck's best friend, Chuck, who shared the same birthdate and was a fellow musician, to get the rest of the musical talent together.

I then contacted all the churches Buck had served as lead guitarist over the years. I also reached out to the music ministers and choir directors, inviting their choirs to participate, via letter and phone call. The letter also requested that each guest bring a canned good to feed the unfortunate throughout Chicagoland.

Then I waited. The responses were overwhelming. So many people came alongside me to make this special day happen. Keshia helped with the original invitations, and she also created the event program. D took care of creating Buck's bio and his musical history.

That left me to reach out to a videographer whose work I'd seen, and whose rates didn't break the bank, and to find the caterer. The contracts were signed. The menu was chosen. And the cake was designed. It was guitar-themed, of course.

All the while, my angel had no idea anything was going on. We'd decided the event would be black and white, so I was getting up in the middle of the night to secretly iron the new white shirts that the men in the family would be wearing.

Now we had to figure out how to get Buck to the event. Once again, I turned to his friend Chuck.

Neither of us worked the day of the event, because, like I did, Buck took his birthdays off. I had all the event clothing folded and stashed in garment bags by the front door. Since I was always donating things—Buck joked that I'd donate his favorite chair if he got out of it long enough—I knew this was my way out.

I told him I had to run over to my lodge to donate some clothes, and he didn't seem to think anything of it. We went straight to the Salvation Army with the clothes and cardboard boxes for collecting canned goods.

Chuck had arranged to pick Buck up for a birthday jam session, and Buck was on board. When I heard that, I breathed a sigh of relief.

In the meantime, the phones were buzzing with people confirming the time and place of the event. My nerves were doing a number on me. Everything was ready. All I could do was pray that things would go well.

The center was already filling up with familiar faces, all there to celebrate Buck by the time I arrived. At the appointed time, John came walking in, guitar in hand and wearing a red suit. Chuck wasn't too far behind. The room was quiet; John just kept looking around in amazement.

"This is for you, baby," I said. "Now hurry up and change your clothes so the party can begin." I sent him off with a gentle hug and kiss.

Jalen went with his grandfather to assist in his wardrobe change. And then it was showtime! My angel sat in his place of honor, still in shock, but happy all the same.

He spent most of the evening on his feet, praising the Lord. I looked around and felt God's Spirit filling the room. This was Buck's type of party—being among the saints, some of whom he'd known for years—worshiping together as one body.

Mixed in with the singing were words of encouragement and plaques of appreciation for the work Buck had done in the various churches. The collection plate was passed around, another sign of love for the man who played lead guitar.

I had the pleasure of introducing the man of the hour and inviting him to the podium.

"Baby," he said, "you are something else! How did you pull this off? I'd better watch you. You could have moved out and I would have never noticed."

The entire congregation laughed with him. He went on to thank the many guests and said this had been his best birthday ever. He would forever be grateful to God and His people.

Right then then and there, he broke into song, serenading me by singing, "Rock me baby, I am going to rock you all night long, rock me like I ain't got no bone."

He took me by my hand and twirled me around, telling the congregation, "See, look at what I got. She is all that, my wife. God is good."

Pastor Stokes closed us out with a benediction, but not before cracking some jokes of his own. After that, he spoke about the type of man Buck was—a friend and a man seeking after God.

My angel was all over the place that night, hugging and laughing. He didn't stop talking the whole drive home.

Thirty-Two Years Married

That which we have seen and heard declare we unto you,
that ye also may have fellowship with us: and truly our fel-
lowship is with the Father, and with his Son Jesus Christ.
—1 John 1:3

Buck and I were driving to work together as the date approached, when my angel brought up the subject of our thirty-second anniversary and asked me how I wanted to celebrate. I asked him what he wanted to do. He didn't think about it long before he said with excitement, "Why don't we renew our wedding vows?"

I felt my heart flutter, while my face lit up with joy. Of all the ways we could celebrate, the man of my dreams wanted to celebrate our love for each other by renewing our love and commitment to each other again for life, this time in Las Vegas.

I couldn't focus on work at all that day. I just wanted to plan our anniversary trip. I'd had been to Vegas before, with one of my sisters, but Buck hadn't. I knew he'd want to see the city.

Later that day, I called up a travel agent we'd used before and explained to her what I was looking for. She got back with me within an hour or so, and we talked about what she had found for a hotel and airfare package. I knew of the hotel she recommended, so after a short talk with Baby, we agreed on it and it was a go.

We hadn't had a wedding when we first got married, just a simple marriage ceremony, which we considered one of the highlights of our lives.

Still, I'd never gotten to wear the white dress or meet my husband in a little chapel. Now was my chance. I started looking for the perfect chapel, which was no easy feat in Las Vegas. I did most of my searching online, and I couldn't believe what most of the chapels looked like. People thought these gaudy things were romantic?

It took me about three weeks before I found the perfect chapel. The seats were draped with white, and it had flowers along the aisles. The room had gold accents, white walls, and a very airy atmosphere. Outside, it had a garden with a waterfall, a gazebo, and a brook running under a bridge.

The plans were set. We'd renew our vows thirty-two years to the day of first saying "I do."

The chapel provided us with a limousine the day of our vows. The sun was shining brightly, and a gentle breeze was blowing. I exited the limo in awe, looking at the chapel. It was more beautiful to my eyes in real time. My angel was in awe, as well; this was meant to be.

We entered and were greeted by the young minister and the photographer. We had a little small talk, just to get familiar with each other.

The minister admired our years of dedication to the true meaning of holy matrimony.

He asked us how it felt to be married for so many years. We both looked at each other and said it didn't seem long at all. It seemed like yesterday that we'd first made our commitment to each other. The minister commented on my ring, which he said was beautiful and unique. Buck said, "Yes, just like my wife."

I should say that Buck had gotten me a new ring to

celebrate every decade of our marriage. It was a representation to me of the newness of our love and our dedication for life. It was a blessing that I could increase my circles of love each decade.

And what woman does not like diamonds?

During the renewal vows, Buck gave me the side eye, as if to say, "No jokes, Lady L." I gave him my smile, my way of saying, *Nothing is wrong, all is right.*

My angel stood facing me in his white vest and slacks, looking as cool and handsome as ever. I wore an off-white fitted dress that dropped to my knees. It had a long sleeve on one side and was sleeveless on the other. It was quite an upgrade from the blue sweaters and jeans we'd worn all those years before.

After the ceremony, we took pictures and waited for a CD of the finished pictures to be burned, along with our renewal marriage license.

We spent the rest of the day sightseeing like two newlyweds. We had ice cream and cotton candy. We laughed about being Mr. and Mrs. Buckner twice over. And we felt like kids again. We'd stop other people along the way and ask them to take pictures of us. When you look at those pictures, you see two people very much in love.

I found a blue stone at the airport before our flight home. I'd done some research a couple of weeks before our trip and discovered that this particular stone represented the number of years we'd been married. When we arrived home, I sat Buck down in a comfortable chair and gave the love of my life this precious stone, along with sharing the meaning of it.

Our anniversary was the best of the best of memories,

and I will cherish it for a lifetime. I thanked God for how safe and secure I felt and prayed we'd have many more years like this one together.

After settling down back in our home, there was a refreshing vibe between the two of us. We had a sense of radiance within our hearts for each other, which grew daily. The feeling can only be described as being high on love and contentment. It's as breathtaking a feeling repeating our vows for a second time as it was the blissful morning of our wedding:

John, will you reaffirm your commitment to Louise to be your wife? Pledging yourself to her to be faithful, loving, and honorable. To cherish her according to God's will in the holy bond of marriage?

I do.

Louise, will you reaffirm your commitment to John to be your husband? Pledging yourself to him to be faithful, loving, and honorable. To cherish him according to God's will in the holy bond of marriage?

I do.

Do you promise to renew the vows that you made when you were first united in marriage?

We do.

Do you promise to endeavor to create a Christian environment in your home and to help each other to live godly lives in Christian service?

We do.

Having reaffirmed your faith and love to each other, acting in my authority as the minister, I now pronounce you husband and wife. You may now kiss your bride. I now present,

*for the second time in their lives, Mr. and Mrs. John Buck-
ner.*

I, in all my love and married life with this man, my
husband, have believed that a true and faithful love can be
reality.

I find many people, especially women, don't want to
hear about how a man and a woman can love one another
to the fullest of their being. It breaks my heart when I meet
someone with dreams shattered beyond repair. I grieve
when a relationship ends not in death, but by circumstances. Whether the relationship ended due to betrayal,
domestic violence, mental abuse, or failing physical
health, I can't even dare to imagine the pain and suffering
felt by that wounded individual.

But because of my relationship with John, I know that
enduring love is possible by the grace of God. I am eter-
nally grateful to God for the gift of my marriage to my
angel.

WORKBOOK

Chapter Nineteen Reflection

Read Ephesians 5:31–33.

Marriage is a sacred gift from God, designed to last a lifetime.

John and Louise celebrated their anniversary by renewing their vows.

What did you promise God and your spouse when you said your wedding vows? Do you live up to your commitment? Plan a special date or getaway when you and your spouse can remember and renew your lifelong commitment to each other.

_____

_____

_____

_____

_____

CONCLUSION

He Is the Reason

Now unto him that is able to keep you from falling, and to present you faultless before the presence of his glory with exceeding joy, to the only wise God our Saviour, be glory and majesty, dominion and power, both now and ever. Amen.

—Jude 24–25

So much of my story has been focused on love. As I look back on my life so far, the amazing love of our Savior, Jesus Christ, who poured out His life on the cross to make us His own, stands out most clearly. We are so lost and helpless on our own, but the God who is love made a way for reconciliation in Jesus. My story is a testimony of God's love and faithfulness.

As a family, we can testify that the Lord has never let us down, and that He continues to provide for us in every way. He is the reason that we love to sing and the reason our home is filled with music. He is the reason that we practice hospitality. He is the reason that individual family members are able to forgive each other and reconcile. He is the reason we believe in a bright future for our youth.

We Christians are all called to reflect and share the unfailing love that God showed us on the cross, and I don't know anyone who does this better than my husband, John. He beautifully exemplifies the unconditional love of God in how he treats me and others. In my whole life, Buck is the one through whom Christ shines the clearest to me. A spouse sees us at our very best and at our very worst, and it has been an honor to walk this path of sanctification with John.

Life has taught me that it is important to marry a godly person, someone who has a growing relationship with God and who is willing to love sacrificially, as the Bible calls us to—and then to truly stand by that person, no matter what. It is a powerful, life-changing experience to be loved by someone who truly knows our flaws and still chooses us. I am so glad the Lord led me to choose my spouse well.

The love of my parents and grandmother has also shaped me into the woman I am today. While they have moved on to heaven, I continue to reflect on their advice, benefiting from their wisdom, the examples they set, and how they taught me to be grounded in the Bible. When I look back to my childhood, it is with a heart of gratitude.

My parents worked hard to shape my siblings and me into individuals of strong character. They taught us to choose right even when life is difficult, and to submit to the authority of the Bible. As Psalm 119:105 states, "Thy word is a lamp unto my feet, and a light unto my path."

My grandmother, having lost her husband and being

forced to raise her young sons all by herself, lived through much suffering and many struggles, which hardened her into a woman who could be abrasive and occasionally unkind. The positive side of Grandmama's firmness, however, was that she had a strong backbone and stood up for what she believed was right.

I am convinced that there are many things we can learn from the determination and fortitude of the women of her generation. Perhaps more importantly, while she was incredibly self-sufficient, Grandmama also lived in dependence on the Lord. The woman who loved to sing "Amazing Grace" wherever she went indeed knew how to fall back on that grace.

My mother and I shared a special relationship, often working side by side as I grew up. Since I was her oldest daughter, Mama passed much of her knowledge and skill on to me, teaching me to care for my younger siblings. My mother built me up through her words, teaching me that I am valuable and worthy of love. Mama was incredibly longsuffering, and her ability to faithfully serve my grandmother, at whose hands she had suffered so much pain, is a true testament to the beautiful person Mama was. Moreover, Mama's willingness to serve and love those who persecuted her points to the centrality of the gospel in her life.

Although my parents had their difficulties in their marriage, Mama remained committed and faithful, truly "turning the other cheek" (Matthew 5:39) again and again. In this, she was truly Christlike, and I am honored to be her daughter. Please do not miss this when you read her story: Mama showed sacrificial love in situations when many of us would have been unable to, and the reason she could do this was that Jesus lived through her.

Although my father was impulsive, and his temper got the better of him at times, he took his role as the head of our home very seriously. He was an excellent provider who, while he did not have a formal education, had abundant practical wisdom. Daddy had a strong work ethic and taught my siblings and me the joy of working together as a family. His leadership in the church taught me that there are times when we need to make unpopular decisions and stand up for what is right and true.

My six siblings have been a constant source of support through the years. I love thinking back to my childhood years spent with them—there are so many special memories we share together. While there have been ups and downs in our relationships, I've learned to truly treasure my brothers and sisters, both in the small moments, like sharing a meal, and in the big moments, like supporting each other when facing our parents' deaths. I know I can truly count on my siblings, and I am honored that they are a part of my story.

My children and grandchildren continue to fill my life with so much love and cheer. My daughter and son are a constant source of pride, and it is one of the greatest joys of my life to see my grandchildren follow Christ. Proverbs 22:6 says, "Train up a child in the way he should go: and when he is old, he will not depart from it." Buck and I aimed to do just that, and God has shown Himself faithful once again. We have filled our home with love and laughter, and while there were tears as well, I wouldn't want to miss any moment with my precious children and grandchildren.

Throughout this book, I have attempted to show the reality of our family. I've painted different family members and myself realistically, being open about our flaws as well as our strengths, hoping to highlight both our need for God and the redeeming power of His love in my family. God has done amazing things in our lives, and for this we praise Him daily.

We have been able to love well because we have clung to God, celebrating His amazing grace in our lives. Although there has been conflict in our past, it is important to note that we, as a family, were able to overcome those differences. One of the most important lessons I have learned over the years, a lesson that I hope this book communicates effectively, is that forgiveness and reconciliation are fundamental to the Christian walk.

My life has not always been easy. In fact, there have been times that stretched me beyond what I thought I could endure, like when my father was not pleased when I married the love of my life, the father of my children.

The rift between Daddy and Buck, and the way we were able to eventually overcome it, taught me two very important lessons. First, the resolution of this conflict speaks volumes about the powerful dynamic of family. Family is stronger than the brokenness that temporarily separates us, and it is always worth trying to reach out and build a bridge.

Second, I have learned to persevere and to trust in God. While situations may initially look impossible to solve, we serve a God of endless possibilities who does all things well. The Lord brought about healing and hope when I least expected it, and by His grace, when I look back on my life, I greatly rejoice.

I would like to leave you with this message: we serve a God for whom nothing is impossible—we just need to trust in Him.

Conclusion Reflection

Read Ephesians 4:32.

Family is stronger than the brokenness that temporarily separates us, and it is always worth trying to reach out and build a bridge.

Louise wisely learned life lessons from each member of her family; even those relationships that experienced temporary strain were restored through the power of Christian forgiveness and love.

Do you have a strained relationship with someone in your family? Life is too short to sacrifice the chance to experience restored fellowship with that person. Ask God to help you genuinely forgive. Seek their forgiveness and as much as you are able, try to rebuild the relationship.

_____

_____

About the Author

Born Louise Smith, Louise Buckner has several nick-names: Sister, Lu-Lu, Lou, Big Sis, Lady L, and Moving Star. A Chicagoan all her life, Sister is the second-oldest of seven children. Known for her unique fashion sense and hairstyles, she has a free-spirited personality, stays young at heart, and serves the Lord with gladness. She is committed to family traditions that are rooted deeply in faith, love, and values pleasing to God.

Lady L married the love of her life, her soulmate, John W. Buckner, nearly thirty-five years ago, and she is still in love with him. She has two amazing children and five loving grandchildren who forever light up her world.

Lu-Lu believes that if you give, it will be given back to you. She is a retired employee of the city of Chicago and an active member of Mount Hermon Missionary Baptist Church of Chicago. She is also a member of the board of directors for a Chicago-based organization, as well as a member of the Order of the Eastern Star, a charitable sisterhood, in which she serves on the Prayer and Worship Committee and the Charity Committee. Big Sis gives back to her community by volunteering with the Salvation Army, and she is the CEO of the John W. Buckner Youth Initiative.

Lou is committed to loving everyone as Jesus loves her. Now, she has stretched her faith by embarking on a journey as an author, hoping to communicate that through our struggles and disappointments, there is a Being greater than our circumstances. She is also an aspiring gospel songwriter and public speaker who advocates for the pursuit of happiness for all mankind.

www.ingramcontent.com/pod-product-compliance
Lightning Source LLC
LaVergne TN
LVHW052025080426
835513LV00018B/2164